Discard

+
913
W   White   c.3
    Lost worlds.

MAY 2 3 2008

River Bend Library System

D1071785

LOST WORLDS
The Romance of Archaeology

Other books by Anne Terry White

PREHISTORIC AMERICA (A Landmark Book)

GEORGE WASHINGTON CARVER:
THE STORY OF A GREAT AMERICAN (A Landmark Book)

THE FIRST MEN IN THE WORLD (A World Landmark Book)

WILL SHAKESPEARE AND THE GLOBE THEATER
(A World Landmark Book)

ALL ABOUT THE STARS

ALL ABOUT OUR CHANGING ROCKS

ALL ABOUT GREAT RIVERS OF THE WORLD

The burnished gold mask of the boy king Tut-ankh-Amen

(Courtesy of the Metropolitan Museum of Art by permission of Miss Phyllis Walker)

RIVER BEND
LIBRARY SYSTEM

MAY 17 1967

LOST WORLDS

The Romance
of Archaeology

by

ANNE TERRY WHITE

RANDOM HOUSE · NEW YORK

RIVER BEND
LIBRARY SYSTEM

MAY 1 7 1957

Copyright, 1941, by Random House, Inc.
Printed in the United States of America

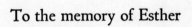

To the memory of Esther

Contents

PART THREE

PART FOUR

Illustrations

Acknowledgments

I AM glad to express my thanks to the Carnegie Institution of Washington for many informative publications and to the Pan American Union for valuable pamphlets; to Dr. Frank H. H. Roberts, Jr. of the Smithsonian Institution for reading an early version of the manuscript; to Oliver Ricketson, Jr. of the Carnegie Institution of Washington for checking Chapter 28; to J. Alden Mason, Curator of the American Section of the University Museum for information regarding the Chama vase; and to Joseph Gaer for a number of helpful suggestions. Most of all I wish to thank my daughters Ruth and Joan for their patience in listening many times to my reading of the manuscript. Their reaction has been an unfailing guide to me.

—ANNE TERRY WHITE

Explorers Among the Dead

ON the 30th of June in the year 1908 the inhabitants of a certain part of Siberia saw a strange sight—a ball of fire hurtling through the air. Immediately afterward they heard loud explosions and felt blasts of hot air. The sky was lit up with a glow that continued for several nights and could be seen all over Siberia and even in Europe. In distant places earthquake shocks were recorded.

"Judgment Day! The end of the world is coming!" terrified people shrieked.

But scientists were quick to reassure them. "A meteorite of a tremendous size has fallen on the earth," they said.

Some twenty years later a group of these scientists set out to search for the disturbing visitor from heaven. They could not find it because the meteorite had fallen in a swamp, but they had no difficulty in determining

17

the exact spot where it had struck; for a distance of 37 miles radiating out from a center, all the trees in a pine forest had been felled. They lay on the ground in a vast circle, their tops pointing outward.

Now let us for a moment suppose. Suppose that meteorite had fallen not in an uninhabited area of swamp and forest but on the populous city of New York. Then every living creature for miles around would have succumbed to the terrific heat and the pressure of compressed air, buildings by the hundred would have crashed, everything that men had created through several hundred years would have perished. It would have been a disaster too great to contemplate.

And yet that same fate, striking in a different way but none the less surely, has been dealt time and again upon this earth. The furious forces of nature and fire and sword and the passions of greed and vengeance and hate have buried beneath the dust of ages vast civilizations that once were the pride of the earth—cities and temples, palaces and tombs, statues and paintings and books, precious stones and objects of gold and silver and bronze and alabaster. You may go east to Greece and Asia Minor, Palestine, Egypt and Iraq, or south to Mexico, Guatemala, Peru, and you will find men digging up the beautiful, sad remains.

These men are not fortune hunters. Once in a while they do indeed find treasure worth a king's ransom, but they are not looking to enrich themselves. They are after something much more valuable. They want to bring back to life the buried civilizations of the past, and especially those shadowy peoples who have lived for us only in legend, in story and tradition—kings and priests and soldiers, and artists, and humble workingmen, who before they vanished from the earth became such creators that their works dazzle us today.

We call these explorers archaeologists—men who talk about things that are old. Their heads are very full of learning. They can read languages dead and forgotten and interpret signs that are just a picture puzzle to us. They can tell under what dynasty an Egyptian statuette was modeled, what age a chip of pottery belongs to, who built a bit of crumbling wall. But for all their dusty learning they are very practical men, whose hands are rough and whose spirits are ready, who know how to work and how to wait. Cheerfully they endure heat and wet and stinging insects and the thousand hardships of uneasy travel and rough camp life. They can pitch a tent and ride a mule and plough through a swamp and push through a jungle.

The adventures they engage in are as varied as the things they find. One scoops out the desert sand and, descending into a tomb sealed for three thousand years, finds a whole museumful of treasure. Another puts on a diving suit and brings up jade and gold from a sacred well. A third hacks his way through a jungle and comes upon cities abandoned centuries ago. A fourth cuts through a hill and uncovers the palace of forgotten kings. A fifth works through a library of clay tablets to find the story of the Flood. A sixth unfolds the secret of a pitch-dark pyramid.

Mummies and dead men's bones, skulls of sacrificial victims, coffins and tombs and sarcophagi hold no terrors for these men. And as for ghosts, that is their job—to bring the dead to life. To make them live as vividly, as fully as in the days before darkness closed upon their civilization and men forgot.

Not all the story has been told. The past is like a shattered jar, bits of which, found now here, now there, have been roughly and sometimes wrongly put together. Archaeologists will have to do a lot more work before all the outlines of the jar are clear. Mountains of earth will be moved, hundreds of picks and shovels and axes and barrows broken. There will be grand adventures, lucky finds. Will any of them, I wonder, dim the glory of Schliemann and Evans and Petrie, Carnarvon and Carter, Botta and Layard and Thompson and all those other explorers among the dead whose stories make this book?

PART I

CHAPTER I

A Boy's Dream

IN the life of every archaeologist there comes a day when he says to himself, "It's no use. There is nothing to be found here. I am just wasting my life turning up the ground." And then he remembers Heinrich Schliemann and digs again. For in the romantic story of the man who found Troy there is a magic that makes men hope again.

From his earliest years Schliemann's thoughts were centered on digging. Most children, of course, have a passion for it, but with Heinrich digging was not play; there was a thoroughly practical purpose in it. The little German village of Ankershagen, where in the 1820's the boy grew up, was steeped in tales of buried treasure, and as Heinrich's father was a poor clergyman with many children, this imaginative child's thoughts naturally turned to gold under the ground. Almost daily he would climb a great burial mound outside the village and wonder how long it would take to dig to the bottom where tradition said a robber knight had buried his beloved child in a golden cradle. Or he would trudge to a ruined round tower and there dream of the treasure that people said lay buried near it. Night would find Heinrich still dreaming of treasure chest and golden cradle. And when from his bed he would stare through the darkness over the garden and across the pond, it was with the hope of catching sight of the maiden who at midnight was supposed to rise from its depths, holding in her hands a silver bowl.

"Poverty is the curse of our life," his father would say when things got pressing.

"Then why don't you dig up the golden cradle or fish up the silver bowl and get rich?" Heinrich would ask earnestly.

When he was seven, an interest came into his life, however, that quickly pushed the treasure chest, the golden cradle and the silver bowl into second place. His father began the boy's education with the story of the Trojan War, and Heinrich, whose passion for the strange and mysterious had already led him to pore through a Greek mythology, heard now for the first time about Hector and Achilles, Priam and Agamemnon, Helen and Andromache. He was enchanted, he begged for more and more.

His father told him how Zeus, king of the gods, feared the growing power of men on earth and determined to reduce their numbers by a war; how he set Hera, Athene and Aphrodite quarreling over a golden apple in order that they might start trouble among their followers on earth; how Paris, son of King Priam of Troy, broke the sacred laws of hospitality and carried off fair-haired Helen, Menelaus' wife, and how Menelaus stirred up all the Achaean chieftains to bring his Helen back; how after long preparation they sailed off in a thousand ships to distant Troy; how for ten years they vainly besieged the city, and how the strategem of the wooden horse gave Troy into their hands; how they set fire to sacred Ilios and carried off Priam's queen and Hector's wife and fair-haired Helen; how Agamemnon, leader of all the Achaeans, was murdered in golden Mycenae; and how Odysseus, shipwrecked on the homeward journey, after ten years' wandering reached Ithaca alone of all his men.

All these stories Heinrich heard, then ran off to tell them to the daughters of a neighboring farmer, two little girls who were his bosom friends and who shared his confidence in the matter of the buried treasures. Together they would go off to the burial mound or to the ruined tower, and there Heinrich would repeat to them the ancient tales. The little girls were interested no matter what he talked about, and so Heinrich dwelt on the parts that fired his imagination most, the parts which his father told him made up Homer's *Iliad*. He told them how Achilles quarreled with Agamemnon over the captive woman, Briseis, and, refusing to fight, sulked three days in his tent; how, when his friend Patroclus had been slain, he rose up in his wrath and slew the slayer, Hector, another of Priam's sons, and dragged the body behind his chariot; and how the old man, Priam, came to beg his son's body, and Achilles gave it to him. When the little girls asked where this Troy was that he seemed to be so familiar with, he was obliged to tell them sadly that nobody knew because it had been completely destroyed and had disappeared from the earth.

At Christmas time that year Heinrich received from his father the great present of his childhood—a copy of Jerrer's *Universal History*. Now in this book there was a picture representing Troy in flames, and when Heinrich saw the huge walls and the Scaean Gate, from which a Trojan hero was escaping carrying his father on his back and leading his son by the hand, he became very much excited.

"Father," he cried, "you were mistaken. Jerrer must have seen Troy, otherwise he could not have represented it here."

"My son," his father replied, "that is merely a fanciful picture."

"But did Troy really have such huge walls as the picture shows?"

"It did."

Heinrich thought a moment while he searched the picture closely. "If such walls once existed," he said with assurance, "they can't possibly have been completely destroyed. Vast ruins of them must still remain."

So they disputed the matter for a while, and at last it

was agreed that some day Heinrich should dig up Troy. To the father this was just indulgent chat. But to Heinrich it was the turning point of his life. He was not quite eight years old, but from that moment on he never changed his mind about what his life's work should be.

As he grew older the boy came to realize, of course, that the golden cradle and the silver basin and the treasure of the round tower existed only in his imagination, but not so Troy. He could not banish from his mind the picture in Jerrer's *Universal History*. He could not abandon his conviction that somewhere in a distant land under the dust of ages lay those great, indestructible walls which for ten years had kept back the Achaean hosts. Through all the misfortunes which fell to his lot in boyhood, through all the poverty and struggle of his youth, he held to his vision. The wealth of his middle years made no difference. He never lost sight of his dream. As time went on, indeed, and his riches grew, he came to care less and less for business success. There was one thing only that he wanted. He was forty-six years old when he put the world behind him and began to carry out the dream he had dreamed since he was seven years old.

CHAPTER II

The Dream Comes True

IT must not be supposed that Schliemann was the only person whose head was filled with Troy. Scholars the world over had long been puzzling over the problems of Homer. Hundreds of solid books had been written by a hundred solid scholars and still the argument went on. A few men here and there clung hard to the idea that Troy was real, that its walls and gates had actually existed, and that if they only knew where to dig and dug deep enough, they would come upon the actual remains of the city. But the great majority of scholars pooh-poohed all this. They had come to an exactly opposite conclusion. "All imagination," they said. "Homer's story of gods and men is no more real than the stories of the *Nibelungenlied*. Legend, sheer legend, all of it—Agamemnon and Achilles and Priam and Hector and Troy."

The reason why there could be two such opposite

28

views becomes clear to anybody who picks up *The Iliad* and then tries to reconcile what he reads with what he knows about the early Greeks. *The Iliad* is a story of prehistoric Greece, and yet the life it describes, the customs, the objects, are not those of the early Greeks at all, but those of a civilization on a much higher level. We know that when the Greeks first emerged into the light of history they were a crude and simple people. They had neither walled cities nor beautiful palaces, nor mighty fleets, nor powerful kings. How does it happen, then, that this tale, written at that early time about a still earlier time, deals with walls that resist a ten years' siege, a fleet that numbers a thousand ships, palaces that gleam with the splendor of the sun and moon? Did Greece go backward? Was it once such a land as Homer describes and was all the glory afterward swallowed up in darkness?

It was really much easier to decide that Homer had had a rich and fanciful imagination than to believe that the Greeks had once been highly civilized, then barbarians, then civilized again. That is, it was easier until you began to read Homer for yourself. When you opened *The Iliad,* you just couldn't have the feeling that this was fancy. The whole atmosphere was real. In every detail reality spoke. Nobody who hadn't seen such things could have described the metal arms of the Greek heroes, the polished helmets with horsehair plumes of various colors, the inwrought breastplates, the greaves with silver fastenings, the shields richly wrought and

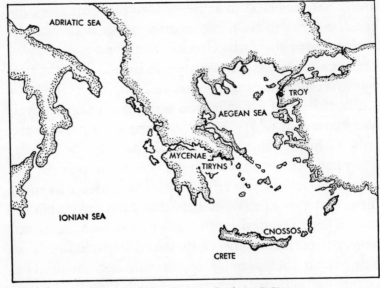

Map of Greece and Asia Minor

decorated. Especially the shield of Achilles. That certainly was something that could not have been spun out of thin air. The man who told in such minute detail about the scenes depicted on it, who described so clearly just how the various metals were inlaid to get the colors desired, had not created all this out of his imagination. He had seen such a shield himself.

It was all very puzzling and contradictory, and the heads of scholars buzzed with it. They argued back and forth about it. They wrote long papers about the problems of the Homeric poems and read them before historical societies. But they didn't clear up anything.

As for Heinrich Schliemann, all the learned arguments had no effect on him whatsoever. Troy had existed for him from the moment his father had first told him its story. And in the years between seven and forty-six he had lost not one particle of his faith. As when he had first seen them in Jerrer's *Universal History,* he was still convinced that the walls of Troy could not have been destroyed. The only question for him was where was the most likely spot at which to try his fortune at uncovering them.

Now it was generally supposed by those few who clung to the there-really-was-a-Troy theory that the city had stood on a certain spot on the coast of Asia Minor where now sprawled a village called Bunarbashi. This little village had been selected for a curious reason. Homer had said that near Troy there were two springs, one of which sent forth warm and the other cold water, and at Bunarbashi there were supposed to be two such springs.

Schliemann could hardly control his emotion when he arrived at the Near Eastern coast and saw before him the immense plain of Troy, the image of which had dominated the dreams of his childhood. But the very first glance convinced him that the village of Bunarbashi had not been the site of his dream city. It was much too far away from the sea. If, as the scholars said, Troy had stood on this spot, which was three hours' distance from the coast, how was it that the Greeks were able to go from their ships to the Trojan citadel several times on the same day? And how could the gigantic palace of

Priam, with its sixty-two rooms, the citadel, the palace and court of Hector and of Paris, and the great gateway through which the wooden horse was brought into the city have stood on this little hill?

It hardly needed his investigating the springs—he discovered not two but thirty-four and the water in all of them equally cold—to make him turn his eyes to another site. This was a spot only an hour's distance from the coast, a flatter, much broader tableland in the midst of which rose a hill called Hissarlik. When his eyes rested on this spot, his heart gave a leap. The scholars might have their theories, but nature itself beckoned him to this spot. What a wonderful fortification that hill made! It seemed to cry out to him, "Here stood the Acropolis of Priam!"

But there was another reason, too. On this site of Hissarlik there had once stood a historic settlement dating from the sixth century B. C. It had been called Novum (New) Ilium. Had it been called that because it was built on the site of Priam's Ilium? The men of ancient times had evidently thought so. To this spot, moved by nothing more than the magic glamor of the name "Ilium," kings and emperors had come. Xerxes had sacrificed a thousand oxen there. Alexander had dedicated his arms in the temple. Constantine the Great had even considered establishing his capital there. The Emperor Julian had visited the altars. Had they all been moved by a dream?

Schliemann didn't think so. He went to the Turkish

authorities and got permission to dig. The workmen came. Picks and shovels and wheelbarrows were transported. In April of 1870 the first spadeful of soil was turned.

The work had not long been going on when it became clear that nature had not deceived Schliemann. Hissarlik had indeed been an enviable natural fortification and the Romans, whose ruined city he came upon a few feet below the surface, had not been the only ones to realize the defense value of that hill. Below the ruins of Novum Ilium were other ruins, ruins upon ruins, of how many successive builders none as yet could tell.

Schliemann was beside himself with excitement. "I have discovered the ruins of palaces and temples on walls of much older buildings," he wrote from Hissarlik, "and at the depth of fifteen feet, I came upon huge walls six feet thick and of most wonderful construction. Seven-and-a-half feet lower down I found that these walls rested upon other walls eight-and-a-half feet thick. These must be the walls of the palace of Priam or the temple of Minerva."

But he was yet in the very early stages of the puzzle. The deeper he delved, the more complicated it all became. Schliemann had thought to dig up Troy. He was digging up much more. Hissarlik was a perfect mine of ancient lore. Not one but many cities had stood upon that spot. Peoples had lived and died, walls had been filled in with debris and leveled, and one civilization had succeeded another.

Evidently the fact that a city standing on that spot had suffered destruction had not kept the next people who came upon Hissarlik from building there. The reason, of course, was that centuries sometimes passed between the destruction of one city and the building of another. In the meantime many feet of dust had fallen on the crumbling ruins. The terrible lesson of fire and sword was forgotten even as the name of the fallen people must have been forgotten, and new walls ever sprang up on top of the old, to be in turn destroyed and leveled.

Every day the excavation became more exciting. Now a Macedonian tower would appear, now a temple of Athene, then again strange weapons, idols roughly hewn, jugs such as had never been seen before. To find any buried city is exciting enough. To find the city about which Homer had written the marvelous poem that had delighted mankind for nearly three thousand years was triumph unmatched. But to find, as came to pass in time, seven cities—later it was discovered that there were nine, and later again that there were many more than nine—one on top of another was simply staggering.

The eyes of scholars the world over turned to Hissarlik. And not only of scholars. Every person of culture and education lived through the drama of discovering Troy. For to them Troy was not just a prehistoric city. Homer's *Iliad* had been the book on which all of them had been brought up, on which all cultured people of the western world had been brought up for centuries past. As children they had built the walls of Troy with blocks upon the floor. As grown men and women the gifted among them had written songs and poems and plays about their childhood heroes and heroines, had put them into paintings, had made them into statues. For to those who have read Homer there are no men and women like Homer's. Achilles and Hector are of all men the bravest, and Helen of all women most fair.

Which of the cities on Hissarlik was the city of Priam? This was the problem which Schliemann wanted to solve. It was clear enough that the ruins at the top were those of Roman Ilium. It was just as clear that the remains at the bottom, right above the virgin soil, were those of a prehistoric people so ancient that they had not even known the use of metal, all their tools and weapons being of stone. But the rest of the record was not easy to read. And, as it happened, Schliemann read it wrong. He decided that the second city, counting from the bottom up—the city that lay directly over the settlement of the stone-age men—was the city of his dreams. Here three years after he had begun to dig he had found thick walls with a great gate and inside this enclosure the ruins of a house filled with remarkable things. The walls showed unmistakable signs of having been burned, and this fact he took to be very convincing. He immediately called the house "Priam's Palace" and the gate the "Scaean Gate." To be sure, the plan of the city as he saw it was disappointing as to size. His Troy was much too small for the great deeds of *The Iliad,* but Schliemann explained this difference by assuming that Homer had exaggerated everything as poets will.

CHAPTER III

Priam's Treasure

AT bottom, in spite of his wonderful success, Schliemann was disappointed. He had still another childhood dream—to find buried gold. Throughout the three years of digging, his greatest desire had been to discover actual proof that his Troy had been a city rich in gold and bronze. He had laid bare half of the ancient town, he had collected a museumful of very wonderful antiquities, but in the 250,000 cubic meters of debris which in three years' work with a hundred to a hundred and fifty workmen he had dragged away, there had been no gold. He was tired out. The hardships of digging on that site were getting to be too much for him. He set the fifteenth of June, 1873, as the last day he would remain at Hissarlik.

And then, on the day before he was to quit digging there forever, Schliemann found the gold. It was morning. He and his wife—he had now for three years been married to a beautiful young Greek girl—were standing with a few workmen at a depth of 28 feet by the circuit wall close to "Priam's Palace." Suddenly Schliemann's eye was caught by an object of a very curious shape, a copper object from behind which came an unmistakable gleam. Gold! His heart began to pound as he realized he was about to fulfil his dream. But his mind worked faster yet. It was necessary to get rid of the workmen. Nobody must know that gold was there, else all would be stolen.

"Go at once," he called to his wife, "and shout *Paidos*."

"Now, at seven o'clock?" she asked, amazed at his ordering a rest hour so early.

"Quick. Tell them that today is my birthday and that I have only just remembered it. Everyone will get his wages today without working. See that they go off to the village. See that the overseer doesn't come. Hurry. Shout *Paidos*."

When she had done his bidding and come back, he said to her, "Go quickly and bring your big shawl." Already he was feverishly cutting with his knife around the hole in which the copper object lay hidden.

It was not easy to get at. On top of the copper vessel lay a solid layer of ashes and calcined ruins about five feet thick, and above that was a wall of fortifications nineteen-and-a-half feet high, composed of large stones and earth. To get at the copper object he had to undermine the fortification wall, and every moment it threat-

ened to fall on him. But the gleam of gold made him
rash. He did not think of danger.

At last he was able to put his hand in and lift out one
by one the golden treasures. They were dazzling. Their
value was simply beyond price. But at the moment the
excited couple could neither count nor value. All they
could do was to lay everything pell-mell on the shawl
and drag the whole to their wooden hut.

Mrs. Schliemann wearing the "Jewels of Helen"
(From "Schliemann" by Emil Ludwig. Courtesy of Little, Brown & Co.)

Safe in their room, with the door locked, they began
to examine the treasure. It was a great moment. Both of
them trembled as Schliemann hung the golden chains
around his wife's neck and held the rings to her ears.
Now the dream of gold was fulfilled. He, a poor clergy-

man's son from far-off Germany, stood on the soil of Troy holding in his hands what he thought were the treasures of Priam. Perhaps Helen herself had worn the diadem he placed on his wife's brow.

After their first delirious play, they examined the treasure carefully. There were two gold diadems—one consisting of 90 chains—12,271 rings, 4066 almost heart-shaped plaques, 16 idols, 24 gold necklaces, eardrops, buttons, needles, prisms—8700 miscellaneous gold articles in all. Besides these there were a number of goblets, among them one of gold, one of electron, and one of silver, and also a bottle of gold.

How had the treasure come to the spot where he had found it? Schliemann immediately developed a theory. He had found the jewels packed closely together in a rectangular mass. Did not this indicate that they had been contained in a chest? The chest had been of wood, it had caught fire, was destroyed, and had left the treasure in that shape. And did not the copper key, which he had found close beside the treasure, carry out the idea perfectly? He thought he could reconstruct exactly what had happened. While Troy was burning, someone had hurriedly packed the treasure into the chest and had carried it off without having had time to pull out the key. At the wall either the fire or the hand of an enemy had overtaken him, so that he was obliged to drop the chest, and it was immediately covered up to a height of five or six feet with the ashes and bricks of the adjoining house.

It sounded likely enough. But Schliemann himself gave up the idea when he found another treasure a few yards away from the first, and three more treasures on and near the walls of the adjoining royal house. Nobody, he concluded, had tried to save all of these. During the fire they must have fallen from the upper story of the palace.

But however the treasure had come there, Schliemann did not for a moment doubt that it was Priam's. This was Troy. This was the Scaean Gate. This was Priam's Palace and this was his treasure. Nothing could shake his certainty that he held in his hands the very jewels that had once made more lovely "the face that launched a thousand ships and burnt the topless towers of Ilium." To the moment he died he believed he had found the very walls which had first set his childish imagination aflame when he saw them in Jerrer's *Universal History*.

Not until three years after his death was Schliemann's opinion set aside in favor of the sixth city from the bottom, the fourth from the top. This city he had missed. He had missed it because at the point where he was digging it had been leveled to make room for Roman Ilium and didn't show at all except for a house corner and a length of fortification wall which he took to be Macedonian.

But the fact that Schliemann misread the evidence takes nothing from the greatness of what he did. Not to the diligence of his successor, Dörpfeld, who excavated the sixth city, nor to that of the American Blegen who showed that "city VII A" was Homer's Troy, but to Schliemann's faith in the great poet belongs the credit of bringing to life the buried world of the Trojans.

CHAPTER IV

The Grave of Agamemnon

ONE would think that the discovery of "Priam's treasure" would have satisfied Schliemann. But the man who had mastered eighteen languages in his thirst for knowledge could hardly be content with just one piece of excavation.

The truth is that the excavations at Novum Ilium had only whetted Schliemann's appetite for buried treasure. Although he had long ago become reconciled to the fact that the golden cradle and silver basin were only legends, he had never ceased to dream about digging up the riches of the past. It was not that he wanted wealth for himself. He was wealthy enough already. His imagination had not been satisfied; it was still teeming with visions of gold under the ground.

Even before he had found "Priam's treasure," Schliemann had been thinking of excavating at Mycenae, for next to Troy it was to him the most important city in the world. There Agamemnon, king of men, had ruled, he who had been leader of all the Achaean chieftains who warred on Troy. Golden Mycenae, Homer had called it. But it had been bloody Mycenae, too. Within its walls Agamemnon, returning victorious from the siege of Troy, had been murdered by Clytemnestra, his wife, who could not forgive him for sacrificing their daughter to the gods in order to get a favorable wind for the voyage to Troy. The terrible story had become the subject of a whole series of Greek plays. It had grown to be almost as famous as the tale of Troy itself. So naturally Schliemann was impatient to go poking about the ruins—all the more because there was also a strong tradition that in the tombs of the mighty princes gold had been buried.

He had already taken a quick glance at the ruins of Mycenae when he had first visited the Greek mainland and had even then decided some day to try his fortune there. Mycenae looked promising. Great underground tombs, shaped like beehives, had been seen on the surrounding slopes; and on the main hill, besides a gate carved with lions, stood the broken fortification walls which in places were still fifty feet high. But of the palaces themselves, within the walls, there was no trace. For thousands of years the winds that had blown over the hill had silted dust into the ruins. Now the whole was overgrown with little shrubs. The peasant Greeks who pastured their sheep on the hilltop knew as little of Mycenae as they did of Agamemnon.

Gate of the Lions at Mycenae

"Giants built these walls," they told Schliemann, pointing out the huge stones that really did look as if some Cyclops had fitted them together. "Over there are the ovens in which they used to bake their bread." And as they spoke of ovens, they pointed to the beehive tombs.

Schliemann laughed. "These walls were the walls of Mycenae," he told the peasants. "Up on that hill stood the palace of Agamemnon. Through that gate the king marched with his soldiers to battle. Some day soon I shall come and show you."

He took advantage of the first opportunity. The work at Troy had come to a standstill temporarily because the Turkish authorities were disputing with Schliemann about "Priam's treasure." They were terribly excited about the jewels the German had dug up under their noses and they wanted to make sure he didn't keep any of them for himself; they refused to let him excavate further.

The thing Schliemann had in mind when he began digging on the Greek coast was not the palace of Agamemnon. He hoped to uncover his tomb. He believed absolutely in the tradition of gold in the tombs of the mighty princes, and his confidence in himself since finding "Priam's treasure" was high. He was going to prove to the world not only that Agamemnon had really lived, but also that he had ruled a golden Mycenae.

Now the grave of Agamemnon was a prize that many archaeologists had been dreaming about, and although they had not made much progress in finding it, they were sure they were on the right track. All of them were convinced that it lay outside the citadel walls. Schliemann, however, had already decided otherwise. Just as certain as they were that the tombs lay outside, so certain was he, on the basis of an ancient Greek guidebook, that they lay within. Once again he stood alone, but now the opinions of scholars did not trouble him. He had had sufficient proof that his own judgment and his faith in Homer were the best guides in the world. So with his usual enthusiasm he made preparations, hired workmen, and in August, 1876, gave orders for a great pit one hundred and thirteen feet square to be dug within the walls about forty feet from the famous Lion Gate.

His luck held good. The digging had been going on only a short time when the diggers uncovered a circle of smooth, upright slabs set in a double row. Schliemann had not expected this, but he immediately became more than ever convinced that he had guessed right. This, he imagined, was that "well-polished circle of stones" on which the elders of the city sat for council or judgment and which had been pictured on the shield of Achilles. Within that circle, he was positive, lay Agamemnon.

The next discovery only confirmed him in his opinion. This was an altar, and it certainly meant that there were graves below, for was not an altar a place of sacrifice to the dead? Soon now they would come upon graves. And, indeed, just as he had predicted, three feet lower down, at a depth of twenty-three feet below the surface, there appeared the tops of five rock-hewn shaft graves.

All the workmen were immediately sent off. Schliemann would trust none but his wife, and she, being younger and having more skillful fingers, now undertook the final work of excavation. For twenty-five days, on her knees, working often with only a pocketknife for tool, Sophia Schliemann scraped away, carefully removing the soil which still covered the royal tombs. Both she and her husband were prepared for great discoveries, for "Priam's treasure" had given them some notion of what they might find. But when the five graves lay open before them, the contents exceeded their wildest hopes. Imagination itself could not call up what actually lay within.

In the largest grave—the fourth—were five bodies; in the smallest—the fifth—one only; in each of the others, three. And with the bodies had been buried hoards and hoards of treasure. The first tomb they opened had been partly plundered in ancient times so that the central skeleton did not retain all the trappings with which the dead had been put to rest; but gold was there, for the sheen of golden ornaments glinted in the debris and ashes. The two other skeletons still had masks of gold over their faces, golden breastplates, gold disks and leaves on the forehead and eyes and breast, golden armbands and golden girdles about the waist. But what testified as much to their having been great personages was the fact that their relatives had sent them off to the next world well equipped for any dangers they might have to encounter. Sixty swords and daggers, many of them with hilts beautifully decorated, knives, lances and battle-axes lay near them. Besides this there was a treasure of gold and silver goblets, gold plaques, an alabaster vase, gold buttons and amber beads.

In the second grave along with other objects there were three diadems. But lovely as these were, they were no preparation for what lay in the third grave. In this grave the bodies—all of women—were literally laden with gold and jewels. Besides rings, bracelets, neck-coils, diadems, pendants, there were seven hundred leaves ornamented with serpents, butterflies, flowers and spirals, and numerous gold ornaments representing chrysalises, griffins, stags, and women with doves and lions. One of the skeletons had a crown on its head, and several scepters of silver gilt with hands of rock crystal lay near by.

Schliemann could not contain his excitement. He sent off telegrams right and left announcing he had found what he believed to be the graves of Agamemnon and his family—to the King of Greece, to the Prime Minister, to the editor of the London *Times,* to the Emperor of Brazil, who a little time before had viewed the excavation and had expressed skepticism as to what might be found there. But all this was not nearly enough publicity. He wanted the whole world to know, and now almost daily he sent long reports and articles to be published in the London *Times.*

The world read, and while it marveled, still the treasure grew. The basket which at the end of the day's work Sophia Schliemann carried home on her arm was always filled with priceless gold, and still there was more in the graves. "I have found an unparalleled treasure of trink-

The golden mask of Agamemnon

ets and jewels," Schliemann wrote in high excitement to a friend. "All the museums in the world put together do not possess one-fifth of it." But the workmanship impressed him almost as much as the quantity. "It is impossible to give you the faintest idea," he wrote to another correspondent, "of the richness of the ornamentation of these jewels. It must have taken the artist, one would imagine, five years to engrave these hunting or battle scenes, like an instantaneous photograph, on the rings."

Schliemann never stopped to ask himself whether he had indeed found the burial place of Agamemnon and his family. He knew. He held up what he considered to be the golden death mask of the king and reverently pressed his lips to it. Not even "the Jewels of Helen," as he called the treasure of the graves, meant so much to him. At last imagination was satisfied. What were a golden cradle and a silver basin and the loot of an unknown robber knight to "Priam's treasure" and this, the golden mask of the great leader of men?

CHAPTER V

A Lost Civilization

WE know now that Schliemann fooled himself. His enthusiasm and his faith in Homer had led him to believe he had found the grave of Agamemnon when actually he had found only a grave which late Greek tradition said was Agamemnon's. Time, indeed, was to prove that these graves belonged to a period some four hundred years earlier; but so far as archaeology was concerned, it made no difference which graves he had discovered. The important thing was that Schliemann had taken a second step in bringing to life a lost civilization.

Archaeologists now poured into Greece by the dozen. They dug in every conceivable place. For the finding of the royal tombs had aroused a terrific amount of curiosity. German scholars, to be sure, had little but ridicule for Schliemann, but in England people were filled with the wildest enthusiasm. Had he not proved that before

the dawn of Greek history a great civilization had flourished in Greece? Oh, it was necessary to dig and dig, it
was necessary to explore many other sites. That civilization could never have existed in just a single city. There
must lie under the ground in many places besides Mycenae other forgotten cities, other splendid relics of a
lost world.

Schliemann himself was convinced that this was so,
and while the men he inspired were feverishly digging—
and bringing up nothing but relics of the Classical Age—
he himself, although he was now sixty-two years old,
decided to carry out another hunch. He wanted to dig
up the fortress of Tiryns.

Now the site of Tiryns had been known to archaeologists for a hundred years, but nobody had bothered to
excavate it. The reason was that the walls which showed
above ground had been baked by fire in such a way that
archaeologists were misled into believing them to be
part of a building of the Middle Ages. But Schliemann's
faith was not to be deceived. He had read in an ancient
book about the huge walls of Tiryns and he was certain
they were still there.

His luck proved better than ever. In the very first
summer his workmen laid bare the whole floor plan of
a Homeric palace. There were the courts, the halls, the
doorways. There were the separate apartments for men
and women. And there, surrounding the palace, was the
huge enclosing wall. It was so huge that the palace inside
seemed dwarfed by comparison. It looked as if it had

been buried behind this great towered wall, which in some parts was fifty-seven feet thick and had galleries and chambers constructed in its thickness.

Wall painting at Tiryns showing huntsman holding a hound (Courtesy of the Metropolitan Museum of Art)

It was easy to see that Tiryns had been rich and beautiful. Bits of decoration still remained about the palace—a frieze of alabaster inlaid with blue paste, and wall paintings, of which the most beautiful and striking of all is one representing an athlete and a bull. This painting is a very curious one. It pictures the bull in full charge, and the athlete vaulting over the monster's back while clinging with one hand to its horn.

What the meaning of this strange bull painting was no one could yet understand; it was only the first of several that were later found. But the meaning of the palace itself was clear. It proved beyond doubt that long before the birth of Greek history a wonderful people had lived along the eastern coast of Greece. Perhaps this people had lived there for thousands of years before the Greeks drifted down from the north. But who were these artists who had built Mycenae and Tiryns? What was their relation to the Greeks? And by what terrible catastrophe had all their labor been destroyed? Who had broken through those giant walls?

As time went on and archaeologists brought to light more and more remains of the unknown people, it became certain that they had lived not only on the mainland but on the islands all around as well. In fact, scholars were beginning to believe that the very center of the civilization had been the island Crete. Certainly the legends pointed that way. The name of Minos, King of Crete, had been mentioned in them repeatedly. It had come down as that of a lawmaker and ruler whose power extended far beyond his capital at Cnossos.

"The first person known to us as having established a navy," wrote the first Greek historian, "is Minos. He made himself master of what is now called the Hellenic sea, and ruled over the Cyclades, into most of which he sent the first colonies, expelling the Carians, and appointing his own sons governors." It was for him that the architect Daedalus had built the Labyrinth. It was for his daughter, the fair-haired Ariadne, that he had made a dancing-ground at broad Cnossos. And long after Ariadne had fled with the hero Theseus, the kings of Crete had maintained their power. Did not Homer say that one of the mightiest of the kings who warred on Troy was Idomeneus, King of Crete?

But when the scholars turned to the spot where ancient Cnossos was supposed to have stood, they didn't see anything very promising. The ruins of some Roman dwellings—and only the foundations at that—were all that greeted their curious eyes. There was indeed on this spot an intriguing hill known as *"tou tselevi i kephala"* or the "Gentleman's Head," on which stood some ruined walls of great gypsum blocks covered with an unknown sort of writing. More than one person had thought something might come of digging there.

Schliemann himself had been tempted by that hill and had even obtained permission from the Governor of Crete to make excavations on the island, but the native owner of the Gentleman's Head had been unwilling to let anybody come poking around on his ground. Had he been ready to pay the outrageous price the Cretan asked, Schliemann might have bought the property outright. But he had balked; the man who had for so many years been a shrewd and successful merchant would not be taken advantage of even for archaeology. And yet he had wanted to dig on Kephala so badly that up to a year before his death in 1890 he was still negotiating for the place. In the end the instincts of the businessman got the better of the archaeologist—and Schliemann did not live long enough to find out that he had let slip an adventure that would have added as brilliant a jewel to his crown as any that was already there.

For another ten years were to pass before the Gentleman's Head was to yield its secret to the pressure of pick and spade and to prove beyond dispute that Crete had been what tradition so glamorously hinted—the very trunk of that tree from which Mycenae and Tiryns had branched.

Toward the close of the nineteenth century there arrived in Crete an English gentleman, a scholarly man who was an authority on Greek coins and other things Greek, and who had for ten years been Keeper of the Ashmolean Museum at Oxford. Now he was searching for examples of a writing which he believed to be Cretan. At least Cretan writing was the excuse Arthur Evans gave himself. Actually the thing that lured him to the island was an urge to explore what lay behind the traditions of Minos and Daedalus and the Labyrinth. But he scarcely admitted this even to himself. He had convinced himself that he had both feet on the ground and that he had come for a very practical purpose: he needed to get hold of some more little seal stones inscribed with signs that were neither Egyptian nor Hittite, such as he had picked up at Athens.

It was inevitable that in his wanderings over Crete he

Wall decoration at Tiryns: woman carrying a casket
(Courtesy of the Metropolitan Museum of Art)

should come to the ancient site of Cnossos and to the hill called Gentleman's Head. And it was inevitable that the gypsum blocks should fascinate him. As he looked at the curious writing, seal stones were forgotten. Everything he had ever read about Minos and Daedalus and the Labyrinth came back to him, and he was seized with an uncontrollable desire to dig. These blocks inscribed with mysterious signs invited exploration. He was convinced they were part of a large prehistoric building. "Might not one uncover here the palace of King Minos— perhaps even the mysterious Labyrinth itself?" he asked.

But still the native owner was obstinate on the subject of digging. They dickered and dickered. Evans, however, was determined now not to give up his dream. Finally he managed to buy the place outright. In the year 1900 he started to dig.

CHAPTER VI

The Palace of Minos

ALMOST immediately things began to happen. The ruins were only a foot or so, sometimes only a few inches, below the surface, so that a few hours' labor brought results. First the remains of walls began to appear, then more and more, and after nine weeks of digging there were exposed to the eyes of the bewildered Evans more than two acres of a vast prehistoric building. The onlookers simply couldn't believe their eyes. The building was so vast that already what showed of it made the palaces at Mycenae and Tiryns seem like dwarfs in comparison.

The more they dug, the more there seemed to be. After a year's work was finished, Evans reported that another year would surely see the job through. He would not have believed then, had anyone told him, that he would be another quarter of a century and more digging up, studying and restoring his building and its dependencies, that a time would come when he would look over six acres of ground and see the ruins stretching over all.

What king had lived in this palace no one, of course, could say, but Evans did not hesitate to call him Minos and his people the Minoans. Through his mind ran continually the words of Homer: "And in Crete is Cnossos, a great city, and in it Minos ruled for nine seasons, the bosom friend of mighty Zeus." He could not doubt it. Here on the site of ancient Cnossos he had dug up the very Labyrinth of which the old legends told. Was Minos the name of the king who had caused the palace to be reared? Or did the word itself mean "king"? Was it a title which, like Caesar, had been borne by a whole line of kings? Or was it perhaps the name of the last ruler of Cnossos, a king in whose name the awestruck Greeks summed up all the glory of this great civilization so much beyond their own crude one? On such things Evans speculated as new and newer wonders cropped from the earth.

The general plan of the building was easy to see; it was roughly foursquare, a hollow rectangle, with main approaches north and south and less important ones on the other sides. In the center was a great court 200 feet long and about half as wide, and around this court spread the wings of the palace, which had once risen to several stories and had been topped with flat roofs. So much was simple, but in the wings themselves things looked very complicated. Corridors and chambers followed one another in such endless succession that it seemed miraculous that anyone could ever have found his way through them. In one section of the building, which had been built on a slope, the upper stories with a staircase of five flights were still partially preserved, and there things looked just as complicated. The whole thing was like a maze. Even after a quarter of a century, when Evans knew every inch of the ruins and had come to regard the palace as a "practical workaday construction," he could still understand why visitors to Cnossos always called the palace a maze.

From the outside there had been no indication of the elaborate interior. It had been almost as simple as a palace could be. Homer had described Crete as the land "in the midst of the wine-dark ocean, fair and rich, with the waters all around." Out of this fair rich land the many-storied palace had risen like a well-cut jewel. Its outer walls were of rubble, in part faced with gypsum, in part covered with a coat of plaster, which was probably decorated in colors. In the bright sunshine of Crete the effect must have been dazzling.

Within, everything spoke of comfort and luxury and of a plan of living that had nothing ungenerous about it. From the size of the storerooms alone Evans could tell that. One section of the basement was given over to rows upon rows of jars, so huge that the Forty Thieves might have hidden in them, and all gracefully ornamented with a spiral design or with a rope-work pattern that imitated the actual rope "cradles" which had been

Huge oil jars and lead-lined pits in the palace of Mino

used in the transport of these jars. Oil had apparently been a principal source of wealth to the Minoan princes. It had been shipped perhaps as far as Egypt. Evans took the trouble to calculate how much must have been stored in these magazines and concluded that there was room for 16,800 gallons! Yet oil was only one of the things that had been kept in this storage section. For more precious things safer provision had been made in the flooring itself. In between the rows of jars were rows of square, lead-lined pits, all empty now, but clearly showing from the care with which they were constructed that once they had contained much of the wealth of the Aegean lands.

On the western side of the palace there was an outer court, and it must have been here, in the days when the palace echoed with life, that the townspeople brought their wares to sell to the great ruler of Cnossos. On the projecting base of the palace wall they had doubtless sat in the shade and awaited their turn to bargain. Perhaps in this court, too, the city elders had met in council. This was the outer edge of the palace life; here town and palace had met.

The heart of the building was its own great central court. In the rooms off the eastern side of this court stood all sorts of workshops where the palace had taken care of its own needs—pressed its own oil, made its own jars, painted its own pots, done its own metal work. There, too, was the domestic part of the palace over which the queen had reigned. Her apartment had been the principal chamber in this section and, with its columns, its raised seats and paintings, by far the most charming in the whole palace. It was a place made for joy. Light streamed into it indirectly from two light wells, and its walls were gay with spiral work and with paintings of dolphins playing in the sea and girls dancing. All the more formal rooms for state and religious use were on the opposite or western side of the court.

The discovery of the throne room in this western section was one of the great thrills of excavation at Cnossos. The first notion the excavator had that the diggers had come upon something exceptional was when the spades struck against the top of the high-backed gypsum throne and its curves began to show above the debris. In great excitement they dug the prize out and cleared the space around it. Nothing in the room had been moved. The big chair still stood in place against the wall. The stone benches on which the counselors had sat still flanked the throne on either side and ran along three sides of the room, the fourth, probably curtained in the great days, opening into an anteroom. On the floor of the throne room lay a shattered, overturned oil jar and some broken libation vessels. An opening in the wall opposite the anteroom led to an inner chamber, which a shrine of the Great Mother Goddess of Crete declared to be a Holy of Holies.

It was a small and simple room, this room in which stood the oldest throne in the world, but Evans very soon recognized that it must once have been a rarely beautiful one. The walls still bore traces of vivid paintings, and down in the trash that packed the floor there were bits of all sorts of gay decorative materials—gold foil and crystal and green porcelain and lapis lazuli.

The throne room of Minos in process of restoration

Evans was so charmed with the place that he wanted it to live again. He had a skilled artist restore the paintings and now we can see the room much as it used to look in the days when a king sat on the throne. A frieze runs along the walls from the level of the benches upward. The upper part shows a rocky scene. In the lower section are brilliantly colored griffins. Two guard either side of the entrance to the Mother Goddess, and two face the throne on either side, as if keeping watch over the Priest King.

For it seems that the kings of Cnossos were priests as well and their palace a temple. The shrine beyond the throne room was not the only place of worship in the palace. Opening out of the same side of the central court were two small connecting rooms, in the center of each of which there stood a pillar made of four gypsum blocks, each block marked with the sign of the Labrys or Double-Axe, emblem of the great Minoan Goddess. This curious sign seems to have been used by the Minoans as the cross is used in the Christian religion. It appeared again and again throughout the palace—on walls, on blocks, on stucco and painted pottery, on seals, in concrete shape on the altar of a shrine, and elevated on a stepped base in the queen's *megaron*. It so far outnumbered all other marks on the palace walls put together that Evans came to call the great goddess "Lady of the Double-Axe."

Worship of the Divine Lady was evidently an important thing in the life of the palace. A large part of the west wing was little more than a conglomeration of shrines, and obviously the throne room itself was designed for religious use. Perhaps the king himself was regarded as a sort of god. Perhaps, as Evans put it, he sat on his throne "as the Son on Earth of the Great Mother of the island mysteries."

What those mysteries were we scarcely know. But that the Minoan religion was not a somber one that worried about life after death, nobody who takes a stroll through the palace can doubt. All the emphasis seems to have been on the good life here on earth, on pleasure, on beauty, on interest, on charm, on comfort. The palace was riotous with color—red-ocher, yellow, black, light and dark blue. All the objects, even those for everyday, practical use like the jars of the storeroom, were beautiful. From one object alone, the king's gameboard, which was found on the floor of a corridor, it was possible to judge the delight these people had taken in color and sparkle and their concern with having a good time. The game-board was a blaze of gold and silver and ivory and crystal. A man who had amused himself with such a toy could not have belittled the things of earth. Nor did the outdoor theater area, with stone steps rising on a slope so that every one of the five hundred spectators could see what was going on, speak of gloom. Here boxers and wrestlers must have performed for the court's amusement, and here, on perhaps the very "Choros" or dancing-ground that Homer tells us "Daedalus wrought in broad Cnossos for fair-haired Ariadne," the young people danced.

CHAPTER VII

Pictures and Tablets

NO question that the Minoans had liked good times. But the thing that impressed Evans even more was the trouble they had taken to make themselves comfortable, the thought and care and ingenuity with which they had built drains and ventilators and lavatories, shafts for light, sinks, and pits for refuse. The fact that the palace was as big as Buckingham Palace, that it had many stories connected by grand staircases, that its corridors and landings and porticoes were decorated with beautiful paintings on plaster and stucco did not surprise him nearly so much as that the Minoans should have put in sanitary arrangements which many houses don't have today. In a little bathroom opening out of the *megaron,* even a terra-cotta bathtub had been provided for the queen.

There was, indeed, in every respect such a very modern tone about this ancient building that Evans had to keep reminding himself that it had perished around 1400 B. C. The people who gazed at him out of the wall paintings didn't seem to belong to another world. They seemed to be doing the things we do today; they seemed to be looking at life from the same angle. The sprightly-looking ladies in their flounced robes and jackets with puffed sleeves, with a row of kiss curls across their foreheads, had all the appearance of Parisians.

A lady of the court of King Minos
(Courtesy of the Metropolitan Museum of Art)

There they sat in the front seats at the shows, gloves sometimes on their hands or hanging from their folding chairs, chatting away, pointing their conversation with animated gestures. It just didn't seem possible that they had lived thousands of years ago. Evans had to turn his eyes to the costumes of the gentlemen to convince himself that the paintings really portrayed the life of prehistoric Crete. With their patterned loincloths, boots up to their calves, their bodies bare from the waist up, and their long hair done in a crest on top of the head, they didn't seem to go with the ladies at all.

Up to the time that the paintings came to light, Evans naturally did a lot of guessing as to what the Minoan people had looked like. To what race had they belonged? The day on which his diggers found the painted life-sized figure of a cupbearer was a great one for him.

Not even the finding of the throne of Minos equaled the drama of the moment when Evans first looked on a man of that far-off time. "There was something very impressive," he afterward wrote, "in this vision of brilliant youth and of male beauty recalled after so long an interval to our upper air from what had been till yesterday a forgotten world. Even our untutored workmen felt the spell and fascination. They indeed regarded the discovery of such a painting in the bosom of the Earth as nothing less than miraculous and saw in it the 'ikon' of a Saint."

The portrait was that of a goodly youth, holding a long pointed gold and silver cup. His right hand grasped the handle, his left held the base, his body was thrown back as if to show that the cup he carried was full and heavy. He was "stiff with dignity." He wore a patterned loincloth and a tight-fitting girdle. On his left arm were two silver armlets, on his right wrist a bracelet.

He looked like no human being Evans had ever seen. He was quite dark, the flesh tint being of a reddish-brown, though that, indeed, it occurred at once to

Evans, might have been merely the conventional color for representing males. Anyhow, he was neither Negro nor Semite. In spite of the dark coloration and the curly black hair, the cupbearer looked distinctly European. In fact, the profile of this man from another world, except for his full lips, was almost classic Greek.

Was the cupbearer a Minoan, Evans wondered? The more he looked at the painting the less sure he became. But in time other paintings cropped up, and Evans could satisfy himself beyond doubt as to what the Minoans had looked like—small of stature, dark, clean-shaven, athletic-looking and very narrow in the waist —was this again conventional painting?—with small hands and small feet, full lips, long noses continuing the line of the forehead, and dark curly hair done up in a crest. These were the men who had ruled the Aegean. These were they who had built

Cupbearer in the court of King Minos
(Courtesy of the Metropolitan Museum of Art)

the marvelous palace and created its works of art. They had vanished and all their works had vanished with

them, but the tradition of their great king had remained.

One day, while clearing out in a section near the central court a corridor that had a distinctly ceremonial
aspect, Evans came upon the remains of a stucco relief
of a great personage. His heart beat high as he examined
the fragments, for he jumped at once to the conclusion
that this was a portrait of an actual Priest-King of the
palace sanctuary. The sacral aspect of the corridor alone
led him to believe it, but the details of the painting confirmed it.

Evans, who had often imagined what the great ruler
who had so impressed the world of his time had looked
like, was somewhat taken aback when, the painted relief
having been put together, he was at last face to face with
an actual King of Cnossos. The king was young and
graceful. There was nothing of terror or awe about him.
He did not sit proudly on a throne, or command legions,
or receive tribute, or go lion-hunting. He advanced
lightly through a meadow gay with lilies and reeds.
Strength and majesty breathed in him. His right hand
was on his chest, his left arm—only in part preserved—
was downstretched. On his bare chest he wore a broad
necklace of fleurs-de-lys, and on his head a crown of the
same flowers, topped by three large peacock's feathers
rising in a magnificent sweep.

What had the left hand carried? A scepter? Or had
there been more to the painting? Had the king perhaps
been leading along a sacred animal, one of those griffins,

such as are depicted on Minoan and Mycenaean intaglios, held in tether by divinities or priestly personages?
None could say. But the sacred character of the figure
was obvious. He walked in a field of lilies—sacred flowers—his crown was adorned with the same. To Evans
this, together with other sacred details of the painting,
was reason enough to regard the figure before him as one
who "possessed something more than terrestrial sov-
ereignty," as one who was "the representative on Earth
of the Minoan Mother Goddess . . . Minos himself in
one of his mortal incarnations."

It was a glorious moment for the explorer. Being able
to see the Priest-King face to face was coming very close
indeed to the great ruler. But he would have wished to
come closer yet. He would have liked to know what
thoughts were passing in the king's mind as he walked
through the flowering meadow.

In the long years he had spent at Cnossos Evans had
come so close to the Minoans that they no longer seemed
a vanished people to him. The palace of Minos had
taught him how they had looked and dressed, what food
they had eaten, what objects they had possessed, how they
had worked and played, created and worshiped. But he
had not made the last intimate approach. Only through
their written records could he know their thoughts. He
had found records enough, goodness knows. In his first
year of digging alone he had unearthed a whole library
of clay tablets. The fire that had destroyed the palace
had only baked and made them more durable. But what

the Minoans had said in those curious characters, which he had first come to Crete to investigate, he had almost no idea.

Many a man from first to last has tried to puzzle the tablets out, but it seems as if the mystery of Minoan language and writing is not to be solved in a hurry. There just isn't anything to begin on for a clue. If we could come upon one single document written in Minoan and also in a language known to us, we could get a start. But there has yet been unearthed nothing to give us that start. One man, indeed, jumping to the possibility that Minoan may possibly be related to the Basque language, which is a non-Aryan tongue spoken in a part of Spain, is trying to work out the puzzle by giving Basque values to the Minoan characters. This, of course, is pure guesswork, at least in its present stage. But we need not despair. It is a maxim that any cipher can be worked out, given enough time and material, and, besides, it may well be that the clue scholars are waiting for will yet be dug up from the ground.

CHAPTER VIII

Theseus and the Minotaur

THE puzzle of Minoan writing was by no means the only one which bothered Evans as year by year he labored to bring the palace of Minos back to life. The question of who destroyed Cnossos and why was always with him.

By applying to his study the various methods of archaeology—by measuring deposits and carefully noting all that appeared in each layer, by classifying the pottery, by comparing styles of architecture and painting and decoration and writing, by noting all the breaks in continuity and by dating every find which showed contact with Egypt—Evans had already determined that the palace had had a long and stormy history. It had been built not long before 2000 B. C. Several centuries later, about the year 1750 B. C., it had undergone great destruction. Nothing discouraged, the Minoans had almost immediately built it anew, grander than ever, using new architectural fashions, new decorative schemes. Fine reliefs of rosettes and spirals appeared and wall paintings more lifelike than any that had as yet been produced anywhere in the ancient world.

And then about the year 1570 the palace had been destroyed once more, this time by a great earthquake. Of this fact Evans was very sure. The overthrow had been on so vast a scale that it could hardly have been the work of man. A long succession of deposits, often containing objects in an untouched state, had been buried in that overthrow. Whole sections had been completely earthed over. On the upper terrace levels of the east slope Evans found whole stores of clay vessels all standing in place on the floor of the magazines and all buried by the great catastrophe. And from the palace walls huge blocks, some more than a ton in weight, had been hurled to a distance of twenty feet, overwhelming a small house, the home of a stone lamp maker.

But again the palace had recovered from the blow. Again it had risen proud and great, a famous landmark. Then once more disaster had come. About 1400 B. C. the palace of Minos had fallen, never to rise again.

It was these last destroyers in whom Evans was especially interested. Who had they been? Why had they leveled the palace of Minos?

Hints of the destroyers were everywhere, but how should he interpret the hints? How interpret, for instance, the suddenness with which they had descended? For everything indicated that the enemy had struck like a lightning bolt. On the very eve of the calamity a gang of workmen had been busy doing something with heaps of limestone before them. Their tools were found scattered all about, just where they had left them. In the throne room the overturned oil jar and the broken vessels on the floor suggested that the king had been just about to perform a religious ceremony at the moment when the enemy appeared. The same sense of sudden interruption hung over the sculptor's workshop which Evans had found on one of the upper floors. Here where the great carved stone jars of the palace had been made, one large amphora of a kind of veined native alabaster—so massive that eleven men with ropes and poles carried it down with difficulty—stood still unfinished, and a smaller one had been just roughed out. And so with the king's game-board. This precious jeweled toy, left behind to fall later into a corridor and be buried, showed how without warning the end had come.

Again, how should he interpret the fact that the Cretans seem to have had no fear that destroyers might come? They had practically no defenses around the palace. Mycenae and Tiryns were almost buried in vast protective walls, those at Mycenae being forty-six feet thick and even after centuries of ruin fifty-six feet high, while at Tiryns they were fifty-seven feet thick and rose to twenty-four-and-a-half feet? At Cnossos, on the other hand, the sole fortification was on the side of the palace which faced the harbor. Here by the stone gangway which was the front entrance to the palace had stood a bastion with a guardroom and sally-port.

A palace so rich and great must have been a wonderful prize to sack. All sorts of enemies must have had their eyes on it. Knowing this, how could the Minoans have gone about their pleasant living with any sense of ease? What had given them assurance?

"The first person known to us as having established a navy is Minos," the Greek historian had written. "He made himself master of what is now called the Hellenic sea. . . ." Was not here the answer to the puzzle? The Minoans had gone lightheartedly about their affairs, concerning themselves with beauty and comfort and a good time because they knew they were secure. The kings of Crete had been Sea-Kings, their navy had ruled the waves, and so long as their sea power remained supreme, they needed to fear no invader. Only a band of desperate pirates might swoop suddenly down upon the palace, and against such were not their fortifications enough?

But it was not pirates who had destroyed Cnossos; the blow had been too deadly. Stronger enemies had broken down the palace walls. Where had they come from?

While Evans puzzled over this, a strong personal experience put all romancing out of his mind and led him tentatively to accept as the most probable cause of the repeated destructions of the palace nothing more nor less than the furious forces of nature.

The particular district in which Cnossos is situated is exceptionally prone to earthquake. The records show

A vase from Cnossos

(Courtesy of the Metropolitan Museum of Art)

that perhaps no European area is quite so prone. Two serious earthquakes a century has been the Cretan fate for the last five hundred years, the last great one having occurred at Candia in 1856, when of 1200 victims 538 were killed and out of 3620 houses 18 were left standing.

In 1921 there had been some slight shocks and after that the coming of another earthquake was expected any time. By 1926 it was considered as being well overdue, and in the mind of Evans, who that spring was tracing

earthquake action at Cnossos, its imminence had become "a kind of obsession." He wasn't in the least sur-
prised, therefore, when on June 26th at 9:45 in the evening of a calm, warm day the earth started rocking.

He was reading in bed in a basement room of the
headquarters house when the shocks caught him, but,
having a lot of confidence in the strength of the building, he decided he would stay where he was and see the
earthquake from inside. The building began to creak
and groan, heave and rock from side to side till it seemed
as if it must collapse. Small objects were thrown about,
a full pail of water was splashed nearly empty. In fact it
was so much like being in a storm at sea that although
the shock lasted only a minute and a quarter, Evans began to get seasick. And to make things more terrifying,
a dull sound rose from the ground "like the muffled roar
of an angry bull."

When it was over Evans rushed out to find out what
had happened elsewhere. He was not worried about his
reconstructions of the palace—he had restored everything he could, spending his personal fortune on it—because wherever possible he had used concrete and hidden steel girders to protect the building in just such an
emergency. He was concerned about the villages and
towns. And rightly. In the neighboring villages the destruction was very great, and in the town of Candia,
while the damage was less, fifty houses had been reduced to ruin and two to three hundred had been partly
destroyed.

After this experience it is not strange that the explorer should have abandoned all theories about who destroyed Cnossos in favor of earthquake, followed by fire and possibly uprisings of the oppressed common people. But many students of history and literature continued to cling to an earlier and much more dramatic theory, a theory that had arisen on the basis of hints flashing from certain of the paintings Evans had dug up, as well as from figurines, rings, intaglios and clay sealings which represented similar scenes.

When the painting of the great bull with the athlete clinging to his horn had been found at Tiryns, no one had understood its meaning—Schliemann, indeed, had imagined that the man was "dancing" on the bull. Nor had anyone at first comprehended the meaning of the bull pictures Evans found in the palace of Minos. Certain things, however, little by little became clear. The Minoans had used the great bulls—they were a third again as large as the bulls we have today—for public entertainment as part of a religious ceremony. Toreadors had gone into the arena and at the risk of their lives had grappled with the fierce beasts. Girls as well as boys had engaged in the sport, the idea of which seems to have been to seize the bull by his horns and to vault over his back.

The dangers of this breathtaking sport, so much more risky than bullfighting as we know it in Spain and Mexico, the Minoans had vividly portrayed in a wall painting which Evans discovered in broken pieces on the east

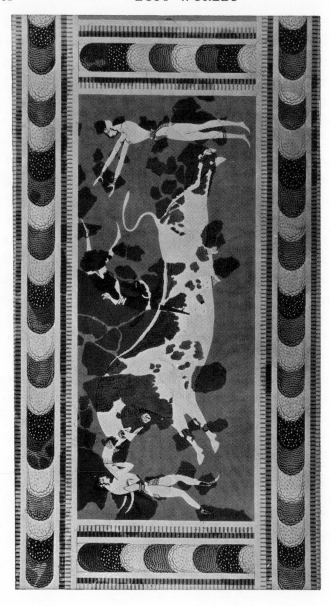

Bull-vaulting scene from the palace of Minos

(Courtesy of the Metropolitan Museum of Art)

slope of the palace site, where it had fallen from an upper floor. The picture is of a bull and three toreadors, two girls and a boy. The bull is coursing at full gallop, and the boy toreador is turning a back somersault over the beast. One of the girls holds out her hands to catch or steady him as he comes to the ground, the other girl is standing in front of the bull. She is just at the most dangerous moment of the sport, getting a grip on the horns so that she too may do a back somersault over the bull. One of the horns seems to be passing under her left armpit and it isn't at all certain that she will succeed in getting her grip and vaulting over the monster's back. It looks almost as if the bull has "got" her and will gore her to death.

Who were these youths and maidens who took part in the death-dealing sport? Did they risk their lives willingly? Or were they forced against their wills to grapple with the bull?

Evans, for his part, leaned to the opinion that the toreadors weren't captives. They looked too noble and elegant and had their hair too fashionably dressed, he thought, for that. But other theorists didn't agree with him. The figures in the painting, they felt, were too reminiscent of a certain legend to be regarded as anything but captives. For was not this palace of Minos the Labyrinth, did not the word Minotaur mean Minos-Bull? And didn't the legend of Theseus and the Minotaur insist that there were captives?

How did the story go?

Once upon a time there ruled in Crete a mighty king, named Minos, for whom the architect Daedalus fashioned a building, vast and intricate as a maze, wherein the king kept a fearful monster. Labyrinth the building was called, and the monster, who was half-man half-bull, was called the Minotaur. Now this Minos had a son, Androgeus, who went to Athens one day to take part in the games and there showed such prowess that he overcame all the Greeks. Aegeus, the King of Athens, did not like this in the least and caused Androgeus to be slain.

As might be expected, Minos did not take the murder of his son lightly. He was enraged, and raising a great fleet he made war on Athens in so devastating a fashion that the Athenians begged him to make peace with them. This Minos did, but on very humiliating terms. Every nine years the Athenians would have to send to Crete a tribute of seven youths and seven maidens to be served up to the monster Minotaur. Bitter as it was for them, the Athenians had to submit.

Now when the Minoan heralds arrived in Athens for the third time to remind Aegeus that the tribute was due, it happened that Theseus had just come to the city. This Theseus was the son of Aegeus, but he had been brought up elsewhere and had now come to the city to make himself known to his father. When Theseus saw how angry the people were with Aegeus for getting them into trouble, he felt so badly that he decided to offer himself as one of the seven youths to be sent to

Crete. Aegeus was brokenhearted to have his newly-found son go, but Theseus was determined. So the gloomy ship hoisted its black sails and put to sea, the Athenians sadly watching them off from the shore, and the last thing Theseus said was that in case he succeeded in killing the Minotaur, he would change the black sails to white ones.

Arrived in Cnossos, the captives were led out and displayed before Minos. And there and then it was that Ariadne, Minos' daughter, lost her heart to the handsome youth from Athens. That night, when Theseus lay in his dungeon, Ariadne came to him and begged him to flee. But Theseus had no intention of deserting his companions; so Ariadne decided to help him in a different way. She gave him a sword and a ball of thread—the sword to defend himself with, the thread to help him find his way back through the maze of the Labyrinth. She herself would hold the ball, and Theseus, with the thread tied to his arm, was to go and seek out the monster.

So it was that the hero met the Minotaur in the dim depths of the Labyrinth and battled furiously with him. Then, when the creature lay dead at his feet, Theseus retraced his steps, and together with his companions fled the island, not neglecting to take with him the fair-haired Ariadne. But the Greek youths were so excited when they came in sight of the city which they had never expected to see again that they forgot all about hoisting the white sails, and Aegeus, believing his son to have been devoured, cast himself into the sea, whence it is called Aegean to this day.

Now this story of Theseus and the Minotaur was one of the legends that was most firmly believed in by the Greeks. Indeed, they regarded it with something of awe. They actually came to believe that a certain old ship they had was the very one Theseus had sailed in to Crete, and every year they used to send this ship with special sacrifices to Delos. While the ship was away, Athens remained in a state of solemnity and would do nothing that might reflect discredit on it. The execution of Socrates, for example, was postponed for thirty days till the sacred ship had returned.

Was there nothing, the theorists argued, behind this story that had made so great an impression on the Greeks? Or was there beneath all the fantasy at least a grain of actual fact?

They were sure, as indeed Evans was, too, that the palace of Minos, in its ruin so seemingly like a maze with its rooms upon rooms, its corridors, its staircases and its courts, was the Labyrinth of the legend. Even the origin of the name was clear, for, as Evans himself pointed out, the sign of the *labrys,* the double-headed axe of the Minoan Goddess, engraved in a thousand places about the palace, insisted that the palace be known by the divine emblem. The bull-vaulting painting, said the theorists, gave a hint of the rest. Youths and maidens had perhaps been forced as tribute from the mainland, and though they had not been served up to the Minotaur for food, they had none the less faced death before a bull. And Theseus? His part in the legend was clear. Whether there ever was a hero of that name or not, in his act of slaying the Minotaur, legend commemorated the triumphant day when invaders from the mainland had revenged themselves on Minos and laid his mighty palace low.

It was only with the last part of the theory that Evans, under stress of his earthquake experience, took issue. It seemed to him more likely that the legend of the Minotaur had sprung up after the palace had already been destroyed. He saw the invaders coming to Crete not as destroyers but as settlers. He saw them awed by the vast remains of the palace, which, in its ruined and deserted state, with its choked gangways and great subterranean stone-built drains through which a stooping man might make his way, looked so much like a maze. He saw their imaginations stirred by the vivid bull paintings, at that time still standing in place. And out of the mystery and terror and vastness of the palace, out of the bulls and the toreadors, he imagined them slowly building that legend of Theseus and the Minotaur which was to be so firmly believed in as the years went on.

CHAPTER IX

The Destroyers

BUT what if we do not accept the earthquake theory and tend rather to believe, as many people do, that the palace of Minos fell for that last time at the hands of man? Who were these destroyers? Were the invaders Greeks, as the legend hinted? To settle that question, we have to get a bird's-eye view of what was going on in Europe during the centuries just before Cnossos fell.

In those prehistoric days when the nations that lived all over Southern Europe were yet of that small, dark, full-lipped type pictured on the walls of the Labyrinth, there had begun to push westward and southward a different race of people. Nobody knows exactly where these people came from originally. Some say they came from Asia, some say they came from the region of the Caspian Sea. But wherever they came from, they were of that light-skinned, Indo-Iranian race which inhabits practically the whole of Europe today.

Now these people were at that time much less civilized than the dark-skinned Cretans and the colonists whom they had sent out to build Mycenae and Tiryns. In fact, they could hardly be said to have a civilization at all. They had no beautiful palaces, they had no art, they had even no settled habitation, but moved here and there in nomad fashion, seeking pasture for their herds. And in their search for pasture they pushed all over Europe. A branch of them, the Achaeans, swept down into Greece and there for the first time came into contact with civilized beings. How wonderful golden Mycenae seemed to them! How wonderful the objects these city-dwellers possessed! The nomad hordes had never seen anything like them before and they determined to make them their own. They made attacks, but the great walls held. Then the Achaeans settled down. They began to learn the arts of the dark-skinned race.

What happened next? No one is sure. Some writers say that when the Achaeans attacked again, the Mycenaeans fled to Crete, hoping to receive hospitality from the mother colony, and that when the Minoans didn't welcome them, they burned and sacked Cnossos. Others say that the Achaeans first destroyed the Mycenaeans and then, when they had mastered the sea, they conquered the Minoans. Whichever way it was, and whoever destroyed Cnossos, the blow was too much for the Minoans. They never recovered. The palace of Minos never rose again. Some of the defeated islanders fled across the sea to Asia Minor, where they became the

Philistines who warred against the Hebrew people. A few crept back to the old site of splendor, but they only built rude dividing walls in the ruined chambers and lived there in a very humble way.

What seems very likely is that the Achaeans at last seized control of the Aegean lands. If Homer's tale is based on real personalities, Achaean Agamemnon ruled in golden Mycenae, Achaean Idomeneus ruled in Crete. Menelaus, Achilles, Odysseus, each had his kingdom. They warred on Troy.

Then down came the Dorians, the people we know as the first Greeks. They were of the same blood as the Achaeans, but they were not nearly so civilized as the Achaeans themselves had been when first they came in sight of Mycenae. The Dorians recognized no blood bond with their brothers who had pushed into Greece before them. To them the Achaeans in turn were strange city-dwellers whom they had every right to despoil. And they did. They destroyed nearly everything they saw and learned almost nothing of what they destroyed. They could not create the things anew.

Only for words and bold deeds these Dorian Greeks had appreciation. They listened to the tale of Troy with rapture. The names of Hector and Achilles grew more dear to them than the names of their own heroes. And so the Achaean tale of Troy became their own.

PART II

A Vast Cemetery

IT has taken many a pick and shovel to prove to the unbelieving world that the history of Greece went back long before the year 776 B. C. with which historians used to begin it. But with Egypt the case has been different. Nobody needed to be convinced that it had had a history once great, now lost; the monuments of that lost history were right there for everyone to see. From time immemorial the pyramids, temples, obelisks and gigantic statues had stood in the desert shouting aloud that Egypt had been the home of mighty kings and of a people skilled as no other has ever been in quarrying, transporting and setting up stupendous blocks of stone.

Yes, Egypt is immeasurably old. When no one yet dreamed of the Americas, Egypt was old. When Central and Northern Europe was a savage land, Egypt was old. Two thousand years ago, when Rome ruled the

world, Egypt was old; already its history had been forgotten, already sight-seers were flocking to stare at the
relics of a lost civilization.

A lost civilization to which no one had the key! The
Romans who so admired the monuments knew next to
nothing about the Pharaohs who had caused them to be
erected. When the ancients came to marvel at the two
gigantic statues of Amenhotep III, they did not ever
know whom these colossi represented. To them it wa
Memnon, son of the goddess Aurora and king of the
Ethiopians. When they scribbled verses on the gigantic
legs, it was to Memnon, not Amenhotep, that they in
scribed them. But their admiration was not the less ar
dent for that; even the proudest Roman could not look
on the works of the Egyptians without sensing that the
might of Rome was a puny, passing thing. "Remember
that you are dust. Generations are born and die, cities
are built and ruined, nations rise and fall, but we stand
forever," these ancient stones had seemed to say ever
before Rome was born. When Rome would be dust, the
pyramids would say it still.

It is a strange and wonderful thing that we, who live
at a time so much farther from the Pharaohs, should
know more about them than the Romans did. But it i
a fact. The magic spades of archaeology have given u
the whole lost world of Egypt. We know more about
the vanished Egyptians than we know about any other
ancient people, more than we know about the early
Greeks and Romans, whose civilization died just yester

day. We know nearly everything there is to know. And one of the reasons is climate.

Egypt is the archaeologist's paradise—dig and you shall find. In Egypt almost nothing rots, nothing spoils, nothing crumbles away. Dig up the most delicate carving, the finest substance, and you will find it just as fresh and perfect after thousands of years of lying in the sand as though it had newly come from the artist's hand. The dry desert soil keeps everything forever.

But there is something else—religion. All early peoples believed in life after death and equipped their dead for it. It seems to have been one of the first religious ideas in the world. Even cave-dwelling Cro-Magnon man placed javelins of flint and bone within reach of his dead and decked the body with chaplets and necklaces of sea shells and fish bones. But there has never been a people in the history of the world who believed in an afterlife so fervently as the Egyptians did. The idea dominated their life on earth. It was as real to them as existence itself. And for use in that second life of which they were so very sure, they buried together with the bodies of their dead all the things they could possibly have need of. When they didn't bury the actual objects, they buried little models of them, exact reproductions of the real things.

For something like 4700 years the Egyptians did that. For nearly fifty centuries they kept on depositing in the all-preserving soil everything their great civilization produced—food, dishes, clothing, furniture, jewelry, stat-

ues, ornaments, books. Is it any wonder that we have a
complete record of their civilization? It has been esti-
mated that in those 4700 years something like 731,000,-
000 persons received burial, each with all the trappings
his family could afford. Egypt is one vast cemetery out
of which have come the richest treasures ever found by
man. Even today when so much has already been found,
may you put your spade in any virgin soil and have a
good chance of bringing something to light.

Why did the Romans, who conquered Egypt, never
dig? Perhaps they did not guess the treasures were
there. Perhaps they were afraid to offend the dead. Perhaps they thought it was easier to rob the living. The
fact remains that neither the Romans nor any of the
people who came after them up to quite recent times
thought very much about what lay in the desert sand.
They gaped and marveled at the monuments. They
stared at the curious hieroglyphics and made guesses as
to what the funny little figures meant. But nobody ever
thought of bringing back to life the buried world of the
Egyptians.

Then Napoleon went down to Egypt for his campaign. Napoleon had a vast respect for Egypt. He had
been so impressed with its monuments that when he
drew up his soldiers in battle array before the pyramids
he felt called upon to make an inspired address. "Forty
centuries are looking down upon you!" he had said.
And even before he set foot in Egypt he had made plans
to study the country as no one else had done. Along

with his army he arranged to bring down to Egypt a number of scholars whose business should be to tell the world about the wonders of the land.

That was how all the modern excitement about Egypt began. One of the scholars, Vivant Denon, took his job so seriously that he soon afterward published a *Description of Egypt,* a book which had no less than twenty-four volumes of print and twelve of pictures. It was a colossus in itself and just as impressive. People made fun of it, of course, and some said sarcastically that it was not necessary to write a colossal book just because you described colossi in it, but they were impressed just the same. The whole world was impressed. "If a country can't be described in less than twenty-four volumes, it must really be remarkable," people said.

And then came a discovery which raised excitement to a pitch and sent thousands of curiosity seekers scurrying to Egypt. The land of the Pharaohs became a front-page country. Monuments, mummies and papyri were on everybody's lips, and getting hold of Egyptian antiquities became the most urgent business of every museum.

CHAPTER XI

Hieroglyphics and Ghouls

THE discovery which caused all this excitement was made in the year 1799 by one of Napoleon's soldiers. He was digging a trench when his spade struck against something hard. He dug carefully all around the object and pulled it out. It was a flat stone about the size of a sheet of an opened newspaper and had curious writing on it. He wiped it off, but he could make neither head nor tail of the writing. This much, however, he could see—some of the characters were like the mysterious symbols inscribed on the obelisks and tombs. The soldier decided it was something important. He had no idea that what lay before his eyes was one of the greatest treasures ever found by man.

For this stone—which we call the Rosetta Stone because it was found near the Rosetta arm of the Nile—was the magic key for which scholars had been sighing for centuries. Nothing had intrigued them like the hieroglyphics. If they could only get to the bottom of those curious symbols, the curtain of time would roll back and they would be able to read all the forgotten history of the Egyptians, learn all the manners and customs and thoughts of that once mighty people. But though they had puzzled and puzzled till they were weary, they seemed no nearer the solution than when they began. Every once in a while some scholar would declare he had a clue, but invariably some other scholar would prove him to be wrong or, worse yet, an impostor. There seemed to be no getting at the hieroglyphics. Snakes, geese, lions, heads, owls, hawks, beetles, bees, fish, palm leaves, lotus flowers, people squatting on their haunches, people with their hands raised over their heads, people walking—what did they mean? Circles, squares, triangles, half-moons, knots, loops—they could not make one of them out. One scholar after another had been obliged to come to the conclusion that he was beaten. There was just one way of solving the riddle—they must get hold of something written in hieroglyphics and also in a language already known and try to compare the two.

And now here was the Rosetta Stone, answering the description exactly, a priestly decree written in Greek, in hieroglyphics and in ancient Egyptian business script! The scholars were filled with joy and, when in 1801 the stone was ceded to England and placed in the British Museum, they fell to work on the inscription immediately. Getting to the bottom of the hieroglyphics was a much harder job than any of them had anticipated, how-

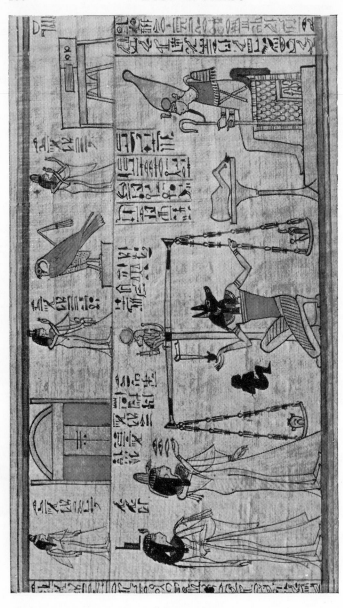

Part of the funerary papyrus of an Egyptian princess
(Courtesy of the Metropolitan Museum of Art)

ever. One after another was forced to give up in despair. But the French scholar, Jean François Chamollion, refused to be defeated. Stubbornly he stuck to the task he had set himself, for he had great faith in a method that the previous work of Thomas Young had suggested to him.

This was the method of working through proper names. The first thing which had struck Young was that some of the signs on the Rosetta Stone were set off in a little frame like this:

When he looked at the corresponding place in the Greek inscription, he saw written there the name of a Pharaoh —Ptolemy. The natural thing to conclude was that in the Egyptian writing the word in the frame was likewise Ptolemy. The signs, he decided, stood for letters, and the letters had the following values.

P T O L M E E S

Of course, this was just a guess. But Champollion, as it happened, was able very soon afterward to put these conclusions to a test. On the island of Philae an obelisk was found with an inscription on it. The inscription was again in two languages, Greek and Egyptian. And again certain symbols were in a little frame. The signs looked like this:

Champollion suspected at once that the word in the frame was a woman's name because Young had already recognized that the marks ◣◖ at the end of a frame signified that.

He now examined the Greek inscription and what was his delight to find in the corresponding place the word Kleopatra. Now he was sure his Ptolemy was right, for the symbols for p, o, l, and e were the same in both words. He had four new letters besides, and now, he thought, the rest would be easy.

He little knew that he was only at the beginning of his difficulties. The Egyptians had used letters only for writing names. Other words they had written in various ways. Some signs stood for whole words, some for syllables, some for letters. The only path open to Champollion was to keep on working with names, and this he did, searching the monuments for *cartouches,* as the little frames were called. It was slow, slow work, and twenty-three years after the Rosetta Stone was found, he had worked out only one-hundred-and-eleven out of the thousands of symbols. But it was a beginning and already the mystery of Egypt was giving way before it. Victory over the whole was just a question of time.

Meanwhile, although nobody could yet read the hieroglyphics, there was so much talk about them that every museum and every curio collector wanted to get hold of some. It was not that there was a vast interest in bringing to life Egypt's past. People simply wanted to possess things, to get hold of them before somebody else did. Explorers poured into Egypt the way prospectors dashed off to California during the gold rush. And the methods they used were not very different from the gold prospectors' either. They did not care what they destroyed in the process of getting what they wanted. They would break open a coffin and make no attempt to note what they found, their object being to capture as quickly as possible the papyrus scroll inside the coffin. They would grab the prized writing and run.

In this ghoulish work the Egyptian natives were only too happy to cooperate. They had always regarded antiquities as the greatest natural resource of Egypt. Some lands were rich in fruits and berries, some in furs and feathers, some in ivory. Their land was rich in antiquities. They considered anything they dug up as much their own as the berries another might pick by the wayside. And even when they were engaged as workers on an excavation job, the smaller antiquities always managed to find their way into their pockets and thence to the pockets of travelers, while the priceless inscribed stones of tombs and monuments would be carried off in the night to build up Arab villages.

Egypt became a madhouse in which there was only one man who cared anything about saving the antiquities of Egypt for Egypt. This was an energetic Frenchman named Mariette, who had been sent to Egypt to buy manuscripts for the Louvre Museum, but who had not been two weeks in the country before he had forgotten all about what he had come for.

Amid the varied excitements of Paris, Auguste Mariette had been dreaming of just one thing—how he might rescue Egypt's antiquities from the ghouls that infested that unhappy country. Almost his first act on arriving at Cairo had been to climb the citadel in order to view the monuments strewn along the fringe of the western desert. The sight of that wonderworld of tombs, stelae, inscriptions, statues had disgusted him with his mission. What mattered manuscripts for the Louvre? It seemed to him the antiquities were crying aloud to him to rescue them. How he longed for freedom and a pick and shovel! And then suddenly chance plunged him into the very thing he wanted to do.

It happened that one day Mariette saw in a private garden in Alexandria a number of handsome stone sphinxes. A few days later in a garden in Cairo he saw more of the same type and again at Gizeh several more. Mariette tried to puzzle the thing out. Was there some storehouse of sphinxes being plundered to furnish ornaments for the gardens of local officials? Then one day journeying through Sakkara he noticed the head of a sphinx sticking right up out of the sand. He got down and immediately searched all around it and became very much excited when he discovered a tablet. It had a dedication on it to the sacred bull of Egypt—Apis! He understood everything now; this waste land was the ancient cemetery where, with ceremonies befitting gods, the Egyptians had buried the sacred bulls in which they believed their god Ptah to be incarnated. He had read in an old book that that cemetery had had an avenue of sphinxes leading up to a temple. He was standing over that avenue! Manuscripts went to the winds. Without asking anybody's permission, Mariette got a handful of men together and set about digging. In an avenue 600 feet long, 141 sphinxes and the bases of several more yielded to his spade.

What a jolt the officials at Paris got when they received Mariette's letter informing them how he had spent their money! But Mariette was indifferent to anything they might say. Already in his heart he had adopted Egypt for his country and in his mind's eye beheld the museum he would found at Cairo. No longer would it be possible for the countries of Europe to whisk away Egypt's antiquities with the excuse that Egypt didn't know how to safeguard her own treasures. On June 1, 1858, he became first Director of the Service of Antiquities.

But even the honest and earnest Mariette had very little idea how to do excavation properly, while as for those others who had the vanity to call themselves "serious excavators," their methods would have turned a modern archaeologist's hair gray. They didn't even know enough to be ashamed of themselves, for the aims and methods of archaeology had not yet been developed.

The man who would develop them was only a boy at this time. Not strong enough to go to school, he was browsing in the library at home, experimenting with chemistry, working out devices for weighing and measuring things. He was spending hours going about the curiosity shops of London hunting up old coins for the British Museum collection, and many more hours making friends with an antiquities dealer, "the most absolutely honest and straight man" he ever met and from whom he was learning more of the world than from anyone else. As yet he only dreamed of archaeology. But already he knew more about digging than the men who were turning Egypt upside down. "The earth ought to be pared away inch by inch to see all that is in it and how it lies," he had said when he was only eight years old.

When twenty years later Flinders-Petrie arrived in Egypt, he was shocked to see that nobody was following this first principle. He seemed to be the only one who understood that the idea of archaeology was not so much to show the mummy as "to show the Egyptian when he was a mummy only in expectation." The waste and spoilage sickened him. A year's work in Egypt made him feel, he said afterward, "it was like a house on fire, so rapid was the destruction going on." His job, as he saw it, "was that of a salvage man," to gather in quickly all he could.

But the destruction was now nearing its end. Petrie had not been long in Egypt when excavators began to understand what he was after and to imitate his methods. It was no longer the things in themselves that were all-important, but the men who had made the things. A new spirit of archaeology was abroad, and before it the darkness in which the Egyptians had for thousands of years been shrouded was giving way to a glorious light.

CHAPTER XII

A House for the Ka

WHEN in 1880 Petrie came to Egypt, the first task he had in mind was to measure the pyramids of Gizeh inside and out. Perhaps if he had known before he sailed what vandalism was going on in that country, he would have chosen some important rescue job instead. But he knew nothing of Egypt then, and looked calmly forward to satisfying on a grand scale his passion for measuring things.

He settled down in an empty tomb to which a previous excavator had fixed a door and shutters, set up a stove to cook on, and immediately felt at home. Every evening at sunset, after visitors to the Great Pyramid had departed, he would climb inside, and stripping himself naked so as to be able to endure the airless heat, would work away until midnight. As yet the world had very little exact information about the way the tombs of Egypt were constructed. When Petrie and the men he inspired and trained had finished crawling around dozens of them, there was to be very little the world didn't know either about the tombs or the men who had made them.

Nearly every visitor who comes to see the great tombs of Khufu, Khafra and Menkaura at Gizeh is struck with the same question. Why did the Pharaohs take so much trouble, spend so much money and exhaust the resources of their country to pile up those mountains of stone? For everyone can see that the great pyramids were a stupendous job to erect. The Great Pyramid alone covers twelve acres, rises even now to a height of 451 feet and measures more than half a mile around the base. No matter how many times you have seen them on pictures, when you actually behold them, you appreciate with a new catch of the breath why the ancients called the pyramids the first of the Seven Wonders of the World.

The key to understanding these man-made mountains lies in the Egyptian idea that the dead man needs his body in the world to come. The Egyptians did not think of a corpse as "life's outworn shell." To them it was a shell that would continue to be used as long as it was preserved. In other words, they believed that death did not break the bond between spirit and flesh; the one was so dependent on the other that it could not exist alone—every step in the decay of the body robbed the soul of some part of itself, while complete destruction of the body meant total extinction of the soul.

Looked at with this idea in mind, the pyramids become less of a puzzle. You begin to understand the whole direction in which the Egyptian people traveled. For with such an idea to urge them on, two things were bound to happen: in the first place, the Egyptians were bound to learn how to embalm the body with aromatic oils so as to keep it from decay. In the second place they were bound to learn how to build tombs in which to keep the mummies safe. They learned so well that they became the greatest builders in the world.

Tombs, tombs, tombs! Everybody in Egypt thought about tombs. That is, everybody who was anybody; for tombs were expensive and poor people could look forward to nothing better than a shallow grave in the sand. Their souls had to get along as best they could. But the rich took every precaution to make sure of a good long life in the world to come. While as for the Pharaohs! Well, the Pharaohs were divine as well as royal, and their bodies were as sacred as a god's, so naturally they used all the brains and skill they could hire and forced all the labor they could command to build themselves such tombs as would keep their precious mummies safe. It seemed to the Pharaoh Khufu just and right and thoroughly worth while to keep a hundred thousand men working for thirty years to build him a tomb that would safeguard his mummy from time's ravage and robbers' greed. All the years he was taxing the wealth and sapping the vigor of his country, all the years he was "grinding the faces of the poor," he was comfortably thinking, "What a long life I will have in the world to come!"

"But how in the world," marvels every visitor, "did they do it? How did those Egyptians ever carry and hoist up those thousands and thousands of tons of stone?"

Not so long ago that question had no answer, and people imagined all sorts of impossible things, chief among them that the Egyptians had a secret method, afterward lost, a mechanical device of some sort which made it possible for them to move great weights. Archaeologists have taught us the true answer. In the tomb of Tuthotep at El Bersheh, dating from about the year 2000 B. C., they found a drawing which shows us exactly how the Egyptians managed. The drawing represents a colossal statue being moved, and there is no machine or mechanical device to be seen. The moving is done by the simplest and most laborious method in the world. The statue is placed on a sledge, which a gang of a hundred-and-seventy-two men drag along the sand. The Egyptian method of land transportation had no trick to it; it relied entirely on brawn.

When it came to quarrying, the problem was solved in just as primitive a way. The Egyptians cut a groove in the rock where they wanted it split, drilled holes along the groove, beat wooden pegs very tightly into the holes and poured water over them. When the wood swelled, the pressure caused the rock to split all along the groove.

The devices of the Egyptians were all as simple as

that. They had none of the mechanical contrivances we
have today, but they did have something we have not—a
patience and a skill such as have passed out of the world.
With all the machines at our disposal in this, the machine age, the most daring of our architects would be
wary of using the great blocks of stone which the Egyptians handled all the time. That is the astonishing thing
—all the time. It wasn't that they performed a few great
feats. Their use of tremendous stones was an everyday
affair with them. You have only to size up the number
of huge blocks in the Great Pyramid or the number of
roofing-blocks in the great temples to realize that it was
the common practice of the Egyptians to handle enormous weights. And as for the stones which they regularly
employed for ornament or sculpture, the use of those
weights is even more astonishing. It is simply unbelievable. The obelisks—those very tall pointed stones with
which the Egyptians usually decorated the fronts of their
temples—and the colossal statues that the Pharaohs
seem to have been so fond of setting around, weighed
hundreds of tons. When you have seen those, you begin
to think that building the pyramids was not a hard job
for the Egyptians at all. It meant merely using that patience and skill of which they had so much.

So much, but far from equally distributed. That is one
of the things Petrie found out by crawling around the
Great Pyramid and getting a headache every night because of the airlessness of the tomb. Although it is true,
as Petrie noted, that "the laying out of the base of the

Moving a statue in ancient Egypt
(An exhibit in the Science Museum, South Kensington, London. Crown Copyright.)

great pyramid is a triumph of skill and that its errors, both in length and in angles, could be covered by placing one's thumb on them," the Egyptians were not all matchless builders. The measurements inside the pyramid revealed many errors. Up to a certain point in construction the architect had taken great care to have his measurements exact, but beyond that point he was often far out of the way. It grew clear to Petrie that two different men had supervised the job, and that the first man had been much superior to the second.

It is almost comforting to know this as one looks at the grandeur of the pyramids. Somehow it brings their builders closer to us when we know that they could and did make mistakes; somehow it gives a living spark to the dead, weather-beaten husks.

For that is all the pyramids are now. The average tourist cannot begin to visualize the life that once surrounded them. He cannot, that is, unless he understands that the Egyptian tomb was not only a resting place for the mummy but also a house for the dead man's spirit or double—his Ka. The Ka passed much of its life in the tomb. It did there the things the dead man had done in life. It ate there and drank there and there it had all its earthly wants supplied. It was quite human and didn't relish being forgotten. Friends and relatives had to keep bringing it things and doing things for it all the time.

This, of course, gave the pyramids a very different aspect than they have today. They were surrounded with motion and color, there was constant coming and going. Visitors would arrive in their boats, moor them near the porticoes at the river's edge and walk up the covered causeways that led to the pyramids. There, in the little temples that stood on the east side of each one, they would deposit whatever they had brought for the Pharaoh's Ka or go on to the pyramids of Khufu's three queens, whose tombs stood east of their lord's. Everybody of consequence came to take part in the cemetery services, and many people of much less consequence came too; for the Pharaohs' Kas and those of Khufu's queens were not the only objects of attention there. Round about the pyramids stood the tombs of the courtiers, and the courtiers' relatives took the responsibility of looking after the Kas of their kin just as seriously as did the Pharaohs'.

But the Egyptians seem to have been so everlastingly haunted by the fear their Kas would go hungry in the tomb that they would not trust entirely to the frail memory of relatives and friends. No matter how a man might be loved in life, it seemed safer to him to pay strangers to remember him. And so whoever built himself an eternal house set aside some part of his lands to pay for food and drink to be offered to his double forever and ever. An amazing bargain! And yet not nearly so amazing as that the Egyptians should actually have got what they paid for. Whoever made the agreement kept his end up. Sometimes for generations and generations his descendants continued to look after the wants of the dead man's Ka, and centuries after the good man had been buried, they regularly brought offerings. Yet even this was not enough, the Egyptians thought. Could anyone be sure he was dealing with a conscientious family? And they found a way to get around that too.

When the explorers first dug out the courtiers' tombs
at Sakkara, they were amazed at the elaborate paintings
they found all over the inside walls. Many of the paintings were about life in the country. Every phase of it was
there. There were pictures of plowing and sowing and
reaping and storing of grain, winnowing and milling,
pictures of poultry being cared for, of beasts being pastured. Were the Egyptians really so fascinated by country life, they wondered? Was that the reason they had
chosen such subjects for their tombs? But then, why did
they have pictures of beasts being slaughtered and
cooked? What was the interest there?

Someone had an inspiration. Why, of course! The
subject of the pictures was the same! It was not "country life" but "food." The Egyptians had caused pictures
of food to be painted on the walls of their tombs so that
their Kas might never run the risk of being hungry. If
their relatives forgot to bring their dinner, the Kas
wouldn't starve anyway; they could look on the painted
food and be fed by the sight!

It may well be imagined with what joy the excavators
pounced on these pictures. They were as good as a
library about ancient Egypt, and they were all the more
to be treasured because the pyramids had proved such
a disappointment. Those mountains of stone had practically nothing in them. A few centuries after the Pharaohs had been laid to rest, the pyramids had all been
entered by robbers and the jewels and treasures that had
been buried with the Pharaohs had been stolen.

Farming in ancient Egypt
(Courtesy of the Oriental Institute of the University of Chicago)

The pyramids were too big, they attracted too much attention. They defeated the very purpose for which they had been made. They promised so much in the way of treasure that it was a terrific temptation to rob them. About the courtiers' tombs at Gizeh—mastabas they are called—nobody had bothered very much. Most of them were too modest to attract attention. The dead man's mummy could not be expected to have been very richly adorned, and besides, it was buried in a little chamber far down under the mastaba, sometimes as much as ninety feet below, which was too far to dig. And in the tomb itself the robbers knew they would not find anything worth their trouble. The mastaba was just a little house for the Ka to live in. All they would come upon there was the dead man's stela—the stone on which was inscribed his name and rank and descent—and his very lifelike statue, standing ready to serve him as an extra body in case anything happened to the mummy. The pyramids, on the other hand, shrieked aloud what wonderful treasures were inside, and naturally robbers were willing to take any risks, work any length of time to get at them.

When the Pharaohs realized this—as at last they did—they decided to change their tactics. They would go in for cleverness instead of size. Since the bigger they made their pyramids the less chance they had of escaping the robbers, they would make the pyramids smaller, but so cleverly that the wiliest robber would be unable to find the treasures concealed within. "You fellows are pretty smart," the Pharaohs must have said to themselves. "You got the better of our ancestors. But if you can get the better of us, you're a cleverer set of rascals than we take you for." And they scoured the country for the ablest architects they could find and set them to outwit their enemies.

CHAPTER XIII

Disappointments and Rewards

NOW the architects had tried a trick or two even when they were building the Great Pyramid. The only way in, for example, was by means of a stone that moved on a pivot forty-three feet up in the north side of the pyramid. But this was to be nothing to the devices they were going to invent. There started now a race between architects and robbers such as taxed all the brains of the one and all the persistence of the other. How far that race got Petrie was to discover when he excavated the brick pyramid of Amenemhat III at Hawara.

This tomb had never been entered in modern times, and nobody knew where the entrance was. Some previous explorers had tried to find it, but all they had managed to do was to destroy much of the brickwork on the north side. To Petrie this pyramid was thus "virgin soil"—there was absolutely no telling what he might find inside; he was not even certain of the name of the Pharaoh for whom it had been built.

He started out cheerfully by clearing the north side of
the pyramid, but there was no entrance to be found.
Then he cleared the middle of the east side. Still no
sign of a door. Petrie looked unhappily at the mountains
of sand and rubbish piled up against the other sides and
decided to give the entrance up; it would be easier to
tunnel through to the center. Even this, however, proved
to be a longer job than he anticipated, and after many
weeks' work he was only halfway through. But at last
the enormously thick brick crust was all behind him,
and before him was the wall of a chamber. With renewed zeal he tunneled through. And then he saw that
his dearest hope was doomed to disappointment. In the
floor of the room there was a hole; the robbers had been
before him.

He did not stop now to figure out how the spoilers
had got in. He dashed to the hole and looked through—
to utter darkness. The hole was too narrow for his shoul-
ders and he could not immediately get down, but after
sounding the water which had accumulated there, he
put a lad down with a rope-ladder. And then by the
light of the boy's candle he was able to make out two
sarcophagi—standing rifled and empty.

Widening the spoilers' hole a little, Petrie succeeded
in getting through it into the chamber. The water came
up to his waist and made exploration difficult, but he
was determined that if he was to find nothing of material value, at least he would learn whose pyramid this
was. The floor, he could feel with his feet, was covered

with rubbish and chips, and these might contain parts of the funeral vessels. His men were not eager to go searching under water, but by promising extra pay to some young lads he got them to poke around with a hoe and lift out chips on its flat blade. It was on a piece of an alabaster vessel that he found inscribed the name of Amenemhat III.

That accounted for the larger sarcophagus. But whose had been the other? In the chamber above, Petrie learned the answer. On clearing this room, his men found a beautiful altar of offerings in alabaster, covered with figures of the offerings, all named, over a hundred in all, and all dedicated to the king's daughter—Ptah-neferu. Evidently she had died in her father's lifetime and had been so dear to him that he had wished to share his sepulcher with her.

There was nothing more Petrie could hope to find, and so now he began to search out and clear the passages by which the robbers had entered. The passages wandered up and down the pyramid and were so choked with mud that in many parts the only way he could get through them was by lying flat and sliding along the mud, pushed by fingers and toes. In this way, sliding and crawling and wading, he reached as near to the outer mouth of the passage as he could, and then, having ascertained where this point was, he could pretty well determine where the original entrance from the outside had been. This spot, which was on the south side of the pyramid, he was able to clear after two weeks' work and there indeed was the entrance which thousands of years ago the robbers had found.

Now that he could follow in their steps and see how one by one they had solved the puzzles the architects had set them, Petrie could not but admire the robbers' persistence. With what infinite patience they had labored till they had found the entrance in the unusual place on the south side of the pyramid! Yet this had been only the first small step; almost at once they had been confronted by another obstacle. A long descending staircase led through pitch darkness straight into a room which seemed to have no outlet. Vainly they had searched the walls and floor; there was no exit anywhere. But their persistence had found the way out at last in the gigantic trap door of the roof. They had broken through this—only to find themselves facing a passage completely filled with blocks of stone. The difficulty had not stopped them; step by step they had mined their way through—only to discover that the passage ended in a dead wall. The passage was a blind, put there to take their attention off the real passage, which all the time had been standing wide open!

The spoilers had now dashed down the real passage, but here a second empty chamber awaited them. They knew what to look for this time, however, and after some searching had found the trap door and slid it aside. Another passage was before them, leading to another empty chamber whose secret had to be found. Clambering out once more, they had found themselves in a passage which led to still another chamber, where now something new presented itself—two wells opened up in the chamber floor. These looked as if they led to the tomb, but they had not deceived the robbers, who had understood them to be false wells, placed there to throw them off the scent. The chamber itself, however, had given them plenty of trouble. It was nearly filled with masonry which they had fruitlessly pulled down in the hope of finding an exit to the tomb chamber. Even this failure had not discouraged them. They had hunted along the passage floor until they had found a filled-in cross trench which they had followed to the tomb chamber. But now the worst difficulty of all confronted them. The chamber had no door. The only way in was through the roof. They would have to raise one of the immense roof-blocks, and it weighed all of 45 tons! Impossible. They could not lift such a stupendous weight. They had had to bore a hole in the glassy-hard sandstone roofing-block.

When Petrie had climbed out through the dark complicated passages and trap-door chambers and come out once again into the open air, his admiration was equally divided between the architects who had contrived the pyramid and the robbers who had solved its puzzles. But he could not at the same time help wondering whether any human robber could ever have found his way to the treasures without some help from the inside. Was it not more than likely that the priests attached to the pyramid had betrayed their trust? Egyptian priests

in later times were known to have regularly connived
with robbers to steal the treasures of the dead. Had not
Amenemhat's priests winked their eyes? Who could
possibly know of their betrayal? None but the Ka, and
the Ka need not give them pause; would it not perish the
moment the robbers had destroyed the mummy?

Bits of diorite and lapis lazuli inlay was all the spoilers
had left to tell the glory of the funeral array; everything
portable they had either carried off or burned. But the
tomb chamber itself they had been unable to destroy.
That chamber, Petrie realized even while he yet fished
uncomfortably for pottery chips, was one of the wonders
of the world, something right out of the *Arabian Nights*
—a huge gem, hollowed out of a single block of hard
yellow quartzite and measuring 22 feet in length on the
inside with walls nearly three feet thick. It was incredible. And its setting was more incredible still. A jewel
weighing 110 tons in the heart of a pyramid! The
thought of it made even this hardened explorer gasp.

How he wished the robbers had not got the better of
the architects! How he wished he might have been privileged to behold Amenemhat in all his glory! And yet
Petrie need not have felt so badly, because the cemetery
of Hawara had a thrill in store for him that would compensate in no small way for the disappointment of the
pyramid.

Among the tombs in that cemetery the oldest unrav-
aged one was that of a great noble, Horuta by name. It
promised great things, and Petrie was determined, in

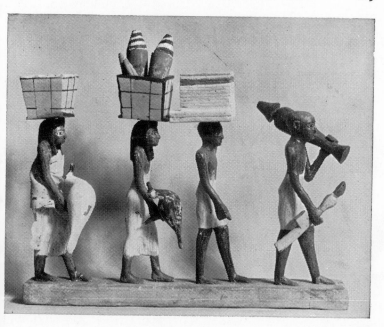

A group of gift bearers from the tomb of Mehenkwetre
(Courtesy of the Metropolitan Museum of Art)

spite of all the difficulties that confronted him, to get the
coffin safely out and for once see the glory in which a
great man went to his rest. The difficulty lay in the fact
that the sarcophagus was in a chamber forty feet under
the ground and partly filled with water, for all the region
of Hawara was flooded by a high level canal of Arab
times. To get at the contents of the sarcophagus, he
would need not only months of time, but almost as
much persistence as the robbers had displayed.

All the work had to be done down a forty-foot well,

in a pitch-black chamber, and splashing about thigh deep in bitter water. In this confined space and under these circumstances, working by the light of candles, Petrie had first slowly and tediously to remove enough blocks of masonry to get at the sarcophagus. After this came the much worse problem of the lid. The sarcophagus refused to open. The lid block was nearly two feet thick and almost under water. It was too heavy to move entire, and so several weeks had to be spent cutting it in two. Then one piece was raised, but as luck would have it, it proved to be the foot end, and though Petrie spent a day struggling with the inner coffins, sitting in the sarcophagus up to his nose in water, he could not draw them out from under the rest of the stone lid. There was nothing for it but to raise the other end.

"So after some days," Petrie wrote afterwards, describing his adventure, "the men raised that enough to get one's head in between the underside of it and the water; and then I spent another gruesome day, sitting astride of the inner coffin unable to turn my head under the lid without tasting the bitter brine in which I sat. But though I got out the first coffin lid, the inner one was firmly fastened down to its coffin; and though I tried every way of loosening the coffin, it was so firmly set in a bed of sand that crowbars and mining with the feet were useless, and it was so low in the water as to be out of arm's reach. The need of doing everything by feeling, and the impossibility of seeing what was done under the black water, made it a slow business."

Wooden model of a traveling boat from the tomb of Mehenkwetre (Courtesy of the Metropolitan Museum of Art)

Finally, since the coffin was not decorated, Petrie had resorted to drilling holes in the lid. Into these he fixed stout bolts, tied ropes to them and then got the whole party to haul till the coffin yielded.

"And then," wrote Petrie, "came the last, and longed-for scene, for which our months of toil had whetted our appetites—the unwrapping of Horuta. Bit by bit the layers of pitch and cloth were loosened, and row after row of magnificent amulets were disclosed, just as they were laid on in the distant past. The gold ring on the finger which bore his name and titles, the exquisitely inlaid gold birds, the chased gold figures, the lazuli statuettes delicately wrought, the polished lazuli and beryl and carnelian amulets finely engraved, all the wealth of talismanic armoury, rewarded our eyes with a sight which has never been surpassed to archaeological gaze."

CHAPTER XIV

Contrasts

GOLD . . . lazuli . . . beryl . . . carnelian . . . "all the wealth of talismanic armoury" had entered with Horuta into his coffin. Petrie thrilled as he noted the position of each gem and glimpsed one by one the fears of ancient Egypt. By what a world of unseen enemies Horuta had been surrounded! What a deal of magic he had required to keep him safe!

For that is what the amulets denoted—they were a safeguard against demons of the underworld that to Horuta had been none the less real because they were imagined. In life invisible enemies had surrounded him. They had made him sicken, they had caused him to die. In life he had used against them all the resources of magic, and in death he would trust to them still. All gems that were gold like the life-giving sun, all gems that were round like the great god of heaven, all that were red like man's lifeblood, all that were green like

128

growing plants—all these were potent against the powers of evil.

Yet even these, Horuta knew, were not enough. The man who would pass safely to eternal life must enter the afterworld with all sorts of magic words, all sorts of magic formulae. For would he not be required first of all to undertake a long and arduous journey in which he would be beset by all kinds of terrors and difficulties— horned vipers, crocodiles, monkeys, monsters, serpents, flames? Only the right words could see him through. And he would need others again when he reached the judgment seat of the god Osiris and the Forty-two Judges, where his heart would be weighed in the scales of truth and where he would be permitted to make con- fession and a final plea. "I have not caused the slave to be ill-treated of his master," he would need to say; "I have not made any to weep; neither have I assassinated any man, nor stolen aught from the temples of the gods or the tombs of the dead."

Oh, there was much to learn before one could hope to attain eternal life! So much that the Egyptians finally seem to have despaired of learning it all before they died. When some of the smaller pyramids were exca- vated, the explorers found inscribed on the walls of the Pharaoh's tomb chamber a long religious text, giving full instructions where to go, what to do and what to say in the world to come. Afterward the middle classes took up the idea and had the texts inscribed on their coffins, while in times later still, everybody who had a tomb took care that the "Book of the Dead," containing all necessary instruction, should be buried with him.

Dying and getting properly buried was certainly a very serious and complicated business that occupied much too much the thoughts of the living. Yet somehow this doesn't seem to have cast a shadow on the Egyptians—not, that is, if people's dispositions are to be judged by the manner in which they live and the objects they surround themselves with. In trying to reconstruct the palaces of the Pharaohs, the excavators found that nothing could have been further removed from gloom. The palaces, although made of a crude mud brick outside, inside glowed with color and abounded in taste. In the chambers of state long rows of columns, carved out of rare woods and gorgeously painted, served as support for the roofs. Doors leading into these chambers were inlaid with gold and silver and incrusted with malachite and lapis lazuli. Many walls were covered with gay paintings, the ceilings and floors were decorated with scenes of wild life in wood and marsh and stream and every piece of furniture and every single object reflected the cultured taste of its master. The Pharaoh and his family—which was pretty large, considering that he had many wives and that his children sometimes ran into the hundreds—lived what we would call an exquisite existence. Everything around them was lovely, and every act of life was pleasant.

Of course, it took any number of artisans, officers, servants and slaves to make this possible. A famous scholar, Gaston Maspero, who for many years was Director General of the Service of Antiquities in Egypt, tells us that the Pharaoh's "toilet alone gave employment to a score of different trades. There were royal barbers, who had the privilege of shaving his head and chin; hairdressers who made, curled and put on his black or blue wigs and adjusted the diadems to them; there were manicurists who pared and polished his nails, perfumers who prepared the scented oils and pomades for the anointing of his body, the kohl for blackening his eyelids, the rouge for spreading on his lips and cheeks." For his wardrobe the Pharaoh needed "a whole troop of shoemakers, belt-makers, and tailors, some of whom had the care of stuffs in the piece, others presided over the body-linen, while others took charge of his garments, comprising long or short, transparent or thick petticoats, fitting tightly to the hips or cut with ample fulness, draped mantles and flowing pelisses." All these clothes, in turn, required in a hot country a good deal of laundering, especially as most of them were white. And then there were the jewels to be taken care of, none too easy a task when we consider the enormous variety of necklaces, bracelets, rings, earrings and scepters which the Pharaoh needed for one ceremonial occasion or another. And, of course, the queen, and all the other ladies of the harem, had to have plenty of waiting women, and for their duller hours all of them needed troops of musicians, and singers and dancers and buffoons and dwarfs.

Headdress of an Egyptian princess
(Courtesy of the Metropolitan Museum of Art)

Yes, it was an exquisite existence, but one that very
few could share. The splendor and luxury of the Phar
aoh and the nobles and the rich middle class rested, i
we are to trust the ancient writers, on the utter wretch
edness of the great masses.

"I have never seen," say certain Egyptian papyri, "a
blacksmith on an embassy, nor a smelter sent on a mis

sion, but what I have seen is the metal worker at his toil, at the mouth of the furnace of his forge, his fingers as rugged as the crocodile, and stinking more than fish-spawn. . . . The stone cutter who seeks his living by working in all kinds of durable stone; when at last he has earned something, and his two arms are worn out, he stops; but if at sunrise he remain sitting, his legs are tied to his back. . . .

"Shall I tell thee of the mason, how he endures misery? Exposed to all the winds, while he builds without any garment but a belt. . . . His two arms are worn out with work; his provisions are placed higgledy-piggledy amongst his refuse; he consumes himself, for he has no other bread than his fingers. He is much and dreadfully exhausted, for there is always a block to be dragged in this or that building, a block of ten cubits by six; there is always a block to be dragged in this or that month as far as the scaffolding poles to which is fixed the bunch of lotus flowers on the completed houses. When the work is quite finished, if he has bread, he returns home, and his children have been beaten unmercifully during his absence.

"The weaver within doors is worse off there than a woman; squatting, his knees against his chest, he does not breathe. If during the day he slackens weaving, he is bound fast as the lotuses of the lake; and it is by giving bread to the doorkeeper that the latter permits him to see the light. The dyer, his fingers reeking—and their smell is that of fish-spawn—his two eyes are oppressed with fatigue, his hand does not stop, and, as he spends his time in cutting rags, he has a hatred of garments. The shoemaker is very unfortunate; he moans cease-lessly, his health is the health of the spawning fish, and he gnaws the leather."

It is an ugly picture. How, we wonder, could the upper classes who loved beauty so much, have been able to endure the sight of all this misery? The worst cruelties do not seem to have bothered them at all. They could see the stick come down every day on the backs of the poor and say lightly with the proverb, " 'Man has a back and only obeys when it is beaten.' If not for the stick how could the pyramids have been built, how could the canals have been dug, how could the Pharaohs' conquests have been carried out?" The sensitiveness of the exquisite Egyptians had nothing to do with pity. It existed only so far as material beauty was concerned.

With beauty they surrounded themselves in life and from beauty they were very loath to part when they died. They were not satisfied, like the middle classes, to have made for their tombs little models of the objects they had used and loved. They insisted on having the actual things themselves, and their insistence proved their doom. Neither size, nor secret entrances, nor dumb chambers could insure their mummies against the robbers' greed. One by one the royal tombs were being entered, until at the beginning of the XVIIIth Dynasty there remained scarcely a king's tomb in the whole of Egypt that had not been rifled. The Pharaohs looked on with dismay, but they could do nothing about it. And finally they came to a desperate decision.

CHAPTER XV

Pharaohs and Robbers

THE Pharaohs had come to realize that if they were going to keep their mummies safe, they must do one of two things—either give up burying their treasures with the body or else hide their tombs from the eyes of man. The first they were altogether unwilling to do. The second required a sacrifice they could agree to only because there was no other way.

The difficulty lay in the fact that offerings were absolutely necessary to the Ka. Thus, while the tomb itself might be secretly hidden in some wasteland far from the eyes of man, the tomb temple must remain in the sight of all. And this meant no small inconvenience to the Ka. Every day it would have to travel the weary miles from the tomb to the temple and back again. This was not a comfortable thought, and before the Pharaohs could make up their minds to inflict such a burden on their Kas, they hesitated a long time.

Radical as the step was, however, they finally had to undertake it as the only possible way to make their tombs secure. From now on they would separate the temple from the tomb. In the City of the Dead across the river from Thebes, their capital, they would raise their tomb temples, while the tombs themselves they would bury secretly in a barren little valley to the north of the cemetery. It was about 1500 B. C. when the new plan was adopted, and for five hundred years afterward every Pharaoh caused his tomb to be buried in the same little valley. It came to be called the Valley of the Tombs of the Kings.

Now the Pharaohs felt they could look forward to a long and undisturbed life in the tomb; for had they not put an insurmountable obstacle in the path of the robbers? But once again they deceived themselves. The really great sacrifice they had been unwilling to make. Like their fathers before them, they still continued to take with them into their tombs a good part of their wealth. With such a prize for the reward of patience, could any robber have been discouraged by so insignificant an obstacle as a secret hiding place? The Valley of the Tombs of the Kings came to contain during those five hundred years a large part of the fabulous wealth of thirty Pharaohs. What risks, what patience, what persistence did not such wealth make worth the robbers' while?

And, moreover, it was next to impossible to keep the hiding place a secret. Too many persons had to know exactly where each successive Pharaoh's resting place was. First of all, there were all the people who had worked on the construction of the tomb. And then there were all the people who came to the funeral. The family and friends perhaps kept quiet about it. But a very small bribe was doubtless enough to tempt a workman who slaved only to be able to eat bread in the sweat of his brow. Once in a while a Pharaoh would indeed order drastic measures to get rid of some of those who knew his secret. Ineni, chief architect of the Pharaoh Thotmes I, tells us, in the biography which he had inscribed on the walls of his own tomb, that he "superintended the excavation of the cliff tomb of his majesty, alone, no one seeing, no one hearing." How had Ineni managed it? Probably by killing off the hundred or so witnesses who had constructed the tomb under his direction. But, of course, it could not have always been possible to get rid of the eye-witnesses in this fashion, and generally the secret must have leaked out.

So long as the throne remained in the hands of powerful rulers, the Pharaohs had some peace. Their tombs were respected because it was not safe for anybody to interrupt the sleep of Pharaoh's ancestors. But when the rulers became weaklings, no tomb was immune. Tomb-robbery went from bad to worse until it was carried on so openly that it was a scandal. And in this scandal the very people who were supposed to protect the tombs took the leading part.

An ancient document tells us that Pewero, the Mayor

of the City of the Dead, was accused of being an accomplice of robbers. The man who accused him was Peser, the honest Mayor of Thebes, who was thoroughly indignant about what was going on in the cemetery. Pewero, of course, denied the accusation. A commission was appointed to investigate, but unfortunately some of the gentlemen on the commission were themselves implicated in the robbery. They managed to clear the rascal Pewero, and the only result at the time was that poor honest Peser was charged with perjury and found guilty. But in the end the truth came out, for eight of the robbers were caught and the facts tortured out of them.

"We opened their coffins," they confessed, *"and their coverings in which they were. We found the august mummy of this king. . . . There was a numerous list of amulets and ornaments of gold at its throat; its head had a mask of gold upon it; the august mummy of this king was overlaid with gold throughout. Its coverings were wrought with gold and silver within and without, inlaid with very costly stone. We stripped off the gold which we found on the august mummy of this god and its amulets and ornaments which were at its throat, and the coverings wherein it rested. We found the king's wife likewise; we stripped off all that we found on her likewise. We set fire to their coverings. We stole their furniture, which we found with them, being vases of gold, silver, and bronze. We divided, and made the gold which we found on these two gods, on their mummies, and the amulets and coverings, into eight parts."*

The investigation now proceeded apace, and it finally became clear to everybody that the entire administration of the City of the Dead, from the mayor to the meanest workman, was thoroughly corrupt. Tomb-robbery was organized as a regular business, and those whose office it was to insure the safety of the tombs were the most deep-dyed villains of all.

At this time the throne was so weak that unfortunately the Pharaohs could do very little to stop the pillaging of the tombs. They seemed to be entirely at the mercy of the thieves. Time and again the priest-kings of the XXIst Dynasty would re-bury now one, now another, mummy of their despoiled ancestors. But finally they lost patience. One of them was so tired of being bothered that he decided to do the burying wholesale. He got together the stripped mummies of thirteen Pharaohs and put them into the valley tomb of Amenhotep II, while into the unfinished tomb of queen Astemkheb forty more royalties were stowed away. And there they lay undisturbed for three thousand years until chance brought them to light.

It happened that a certain poor Arab family came upon the tomb of Queen Astemkheb, which lay not in the Valley of the Tombs of the Kings, but outside it on a height near the temple of Der el-Bahari. Now the Abd-er-Rasuls, as the Arab family was called, were no fools. They knew that antiquities fetched fine prices from the tourists, and they immediately realized that their fortune was made. But they realized also that they could not sell everything off at once because that would arouse suspicion and bring about their own ruin. So they began to sell things little by little. But even so they could not avoid attracting attention at last, for the things they steadily offered for sale were so unusual that the officials guessed a great hoard must have been discovered. And six years later the Abd-er-Rasuls were caught. Of course, they denied everything, but torture is a terrible persuader, and one day one of the family confessed and offered to guide an official of the Service of Antiquities to the spot where the treasure lay.

They went secretly, Abd-er-Rasul, Emile Brugsch Bey—the gentleman who had been sent down from Cairo—and one other person. It was a wild sort of landscape and as they went on and on, the gentleman from Cairo began to think that he had perhaps let himself in for more than he had bargained, when all of a sudden, after a sharp climb, his guide pointed to a deep, black pit that opened up in front of them. Was this the tomb? The guide insisted that it was. And difficult as it was to believe that the remains of the Pharaohs were at the bottom of the uninviting hole—it looked to be forty feet deep and not more than six feet square—Brugsch decided to risk it. He took hold of the rope which Abd-er-Rasul held over the pit's mouth and climbed into the blackness.

Brugsch was ready for anything—except the sight that met his eyes when having stumbled through a partially blocked passage he suddenly turned a corner. There before him was a cluster of mummy cases in such number as to stagger him. In great excitement he pressed forward to the end of the passage. It led into a chamber, where standing against the walls or lying upon the floor was an even greater number of mummy cases, gilded and of stupendous size.

The explorer's heart was beating faster now than when he had taken hold of Abd-er-Rasul's rope. Here were the actual bodies of kings who had ruled three thousand years ago, among them some of the mightiest in Egyptian history, including even the most famous of all, Rameses II, at whose court Moses is supposed to have grown up. It was the greatest discovery of its kind that had ever been made.

But what was Brugsch to do? How was he going to get these precious relics out? Not only was the shaft deep and the coffins very heavy—he later found that it took sixteen men to lift up one of the largest—but he had no laborers whom he could trust. The inhabitants of the village had made tomb-robbery their trade since the thirteenth century B. C. If he asked them to help him, the relics would very likely melt away and disappear before his eyes. But cost what it might, the attempt had to be made, and next morning Brugsch had three hundred Arabs on the spot.

Thieves though they were, for once nothing went into their pockets. The Arabs seemed to respond to the drama in which they were taking part. And when at last Brugsch sailed away with his amazing load of Pharaohs, the villagers rose to the occasion. The women wailed and tore their hair and acted as brokenhearted as though they were at the funeral of their near and dear, while the men shouted and fired off rifles.

It was soon after this that the thirteen royalties who had been stowed away in the tomb of Amenhotep II were brought to light. The discovery was not so dazzling as that of the forty, but nevertheless there was a grand to-do about it, for there was a point of interest here that had not been present in the other discovery. For the first time an excavator had found a Pharaoh lying in his own sarcophagus in his own tomb! It was something so exceptional, indeed, that the authorities decided to leave Amenhotep in peace where he himself had chosen to lie. They felt there was a dramatic justice in this. But unfortunately the remains of Amenhotep's belongings proved too tempting. Three years later a band of robbers attacked the tomb, drove off the guards, turned the Pharaoh out of his coffin, smashed in his chest and carried off the spoil. That, at least, is the story the six guards told. But there are those unkind enough to say—and with evidence to back their words—that the whole thing was staged by the guards, who themselves acted the part of robbers.

CHAPTER XVI

Tut-Ankh-Amen

EXCITED and proud as the explorers were to have found the actual bodies of so many Pharaohs, there was something for which they would gladly have exchanged them all—one single royal tomb that had never been touched, one royal tomb in which everything still remained exactly as when the Pharaoh had been laid to rest. It was the dream of every excavator. In the course of years the dream had met again and again with disappointment, for always the tomb-robber had been there before the archaeologist. Yet every once in a while some lucky "find" renewed the explorers' waning faith and set them digging furiously again.

Such a discovery, on February 6, 1905, was that of the tomb of Prince Yuaa and his wife Tuiu. This couple had belonged to the grand nobility. Their station had been so high, in fact, that their daughter, Tiy, had become the wife of Amenhotep III and the mother of the Pharaoh Akhenaten. Thus, although the tomb had been partly rifled, it nevertheless contained the richest treasure yet found in the Valley, and showed as never before how rich and grand the funeral furnishings were. Every excavator in Egypt thrilled as he read about it, and every one lived through the adventure himself.

"Imagine," wrote A. E. Weigall, one of the directors of the discovery, "entering a town house which had been closed for the summer: imagine the stuffy room, the stiff, silent appearance of the furniture, the feeling that some ghostly occupants of the vacant chairs have just been disturbed, the desire to throw open the windows to let life into the room once more. That was perhaps the first sensation as we stood, really dumbfounded, and stared round at the relics of the life of over three thousand years ago, all of which were as new almost as when they graced the palace of Prince Yuaa. Three armchairs were perhaps the first objects to attract the attention: beautiful carved wooden chairs, decorated with gold. . . . There in the far corner stood objects gleaming with gold undulled by a speck of dust, and one looked from one article to another with the feeling that the entire human conception of Time was wrong. These were the things of yesterday, of a year or two ago."

But the high hopes raised by finding the tomb of Prince Yuaa were soon dashed. A short time afterwards the mummy of the Pharaoh Akhenaten was found, despoiled and hidden in a tomb that was no more than a rough cell in the rock. The Valley of the Tombs of the Kings had by this time been pretty well gone over, and when the tomb of the Pharaoh Horemheb was found completely pillaged, and near it a pit containing objects bearing the names of the Pharaoh Tut-ankh-Amen and his wife, the most cheerful excavators lost hope. "I fear," said Mr. Davis, the American gentleman who had financed the excavation of Prince Yuaa, the Pharaoh Akhenaten, and Horemheb, "that the Valley of Tombs is now exhausted." And practically everybody else agreed with him.

There were, however, two men, who, if they no longer cherished the great dream of finding an untouched royal tomb, at least believed the Valley had not revealed all of its secrets. They were Lord Carnarvon and Mr. Howard Carter.

Howard Carter was an archaeologist by profession, "a learned expert gifted with imagination," a man who had been trained by Petrie himself and who had spent most of his life digging in Egypt. Lord Carnarvon had merely stumbled into archaeology. He had been brought up in the usual manner of a titled English youth—with Eton and Cambridge training (to which he had paid very scant attention) and with an opportunity to indulge every taste. His favorite pursuit had been treasure collecting. He had bought china and prints and drawings, and he might very well have been content to spend all his life in this gentlemanly pursuit had not an almost fatal automobile accident changed everything for him.

After that it was one operation after another and every winter in the gentle climate of Egypt. With his taste for the arts it was inevitable that the excavation fever should begin to work in him. He knew nothing about digging, however, and when Howard Carter was recommended to him as an expert, he was very glad to accept the archaeologist's aid. The two men became friends at once and from then on for the next sixteen years worked together as a perfect team.

Now Carnarvon and Carter were not planning to dig at random in the Valley of the Tombs of the Kings. They were on the lookout for a particular tomb, the tomb of the Pharaoh Tut-ankh-Amen, and they believed they had worked out the very location where it lay. To the eyes of most people their undertaking seemed absurd. Nearly everybody was convinced that Tut-ankh-Amen's tomb had already been found. But Lord Carnarvon and Mr. Carter were not to be dissuaded, for they believed that the pit-tomb containing the fragments bearing the figures and names of Tut-ankh-Amen and his queen was far too small and insignificant for a king's burial. In their opinion the things had been placed there at some later time and did not indicate that the Pharaoh himself had been buried on the spot. They were convinced that the tomb of Tut-ankh-Amen was still to be found, and that the place they had chosen—the center of the Valley—was the best place to look for it. In that vicinity had been unearthed something which they considered very good evidence—two jars containing broken

bits of things that had been used at the funeral ceremonies of King Tut-ankh-Amen.

Nevertheless, when in the autumn of 1917 the excavators came out to look over the spot they had chosen
and to begin their Valley campaign in earnest, even they
thought it was a desperate undertaking. The site was
piled high with refuse thrown out by former excavators.
They would have to remove all that before they could
begin excavating in virgin soil. But they had made up
their minds and meant to go through with it; even
though it took many seasons, they would go systemati-
cally over every inch of the ground.

In the years that followed, they did. They went over
every inch, with the exception of a small area covered
with the ruins of stone huts that had once sheltered
workmen probably employed in building the tomb of
Rameses VI. These huts lay very near the tomb of the
Pharaoh on a spot which Carter and Carnarvon had not
touched for reasons of courtesy. The tomb of Rameses
VI was a popular show-place in the Valley, and digging
in the area of the huts would have cut off visitors to the
tomb. They let it be, and turned instead to another site
which they felt had possibilities.

The new ground proved, however, no better than the
old, and now Lord Carnarvon began to wonder whether
with so little to show for six seasons' work they were
justified in going on. But Carter was firm. So long as a
single area of unturned ground remained, he said, they
ought to risk it. There was still the area of the huts. He

insisted on going back to it. On November first, 1922 he had his diggers back in the old spot.

And now things happened with such suddenness that Carter afterward declared they left him in a dazed condition. Coming to work on the fourth day after the digging on the little area had started, he saw at once that something extraordinary had happened. Things were too quiet; nobody was digging and hardly anybody was talking. He hurried forward, and there before him was a shallow step cut in the rock beneath the very first hut attacked! He could hardly believe his eyes. After all the disappointments of the past six seasons, was it possible that he was actually on the threshold of a great discovery? He gave the command to dig, and the diggers fell to work with a will. By the next afternoon Carter was able to see the upper edges of a stairway on all its four sides, and before very long there stood revealed twelve steps, and at the level of the twelfth the upper part of a sealed and plastered doorway.

Carter's excitement was fast reaching fever pitch. Anything, literally anything, might lie beyond. It needed all his self-control to keep from breaking the doorway down and satisfying his curiosity then and there. But was it fair to see what lay beyond that door alone? Although Lord Carnarvon was in England, was it not his discovery as much as Carter's? To the astonishment of the workmen, the excavator gave orders to fill the stairway in again, and then he sent the following cable off to Carnarvon: "At last have made wonderful discovery in

The Valley of the Tombs of the Kings. Arrow indicates point at which Tut-ankh-Amen's tomb was found.

(Courtesy of the Metropolitan Museum of Art)

Valley. A magnificent tomb with seals intact. Recovered same for your arrival. Congratulations."

As he waited for Lord Carnarvon to come, Carter found it hard to persuade himself at times that the whole episode had not been a dream. The entrance to the tomb was only thirteen feet below the entrance to the tomb of Rameses VI. No one would have suspected the presence of a tomb so near the other. Had he actually found a flight of steps? Was it really there under the sand, waiting to conduct him to the great mystery?

In two weeks' time Lord Carnarvon and his daughter were on the spot. Carter now ordered his men to clear the stairway once more, and there on the lower part of the sealed doorway the explorers beheld what almost took their breath away—the seal of the Pharaoh Tut-ankh-Amen. Now they knew. Beyond this doorway lay either the Pharaoh's secret treasure store or else the very tomb for which they were searching. Yet one thing made them uneasy. They noticed that part of the door was patched up and that in the patched-up part there stood out clearly the seal of the cemetery. It was evident that the door had been partly broken down—by robbers, of course—and then patched up again by cemetery officials. Had the robbers been caught in time? Did at least some of Tut-ankh-Amen's glory yet remain behind that twice-sealed doorway? Or would perhaps only barren walls reward their years of tedious toil?

With pounding hearts they broke down the door. Beyond lay only another obstacle to their progress—a passage filled with stone. Had the robbers got beyond that? They began slowly to clear away the stone, and on the following day—"the day of days," Carter called it, "and one whose like I can never hope to see again"— they came upon a second sealed doorway, almost exactly like the first and also bearing distinct signs of opening and reclosing.

His hands trembling so that he could scarcely hold a tool, Carter managed to make a tiny hole in the door and to pass a candle through it. At first he could see nothing, but as his eyes grew accustomed to the light, "details of the room slowly emerged from the mist, strange animals, statues, and gold—everywhere the glint of gold."

"Can you see anything?" Carnarvon asked anxiously as Carter stood there dumb with amazement.

"Yes, wonderful things!" was all the explorer could get out.

And no wonder. What he saw was one of the most amazing sights anybody has ever been privileged to see. It seemed as if a whole museumful of objects was in that room. Three gilt couches, their sides carved in the form of monstrous animals, and two statues of a king, facing each other like two sentinels, were the most prominent things in the room, but all around and between were hosts of other things—inlaid caskets, alabaster vases, shrines, beds, chairs, a golden inlaid throne, a heap of white boxes (which they later found were filled with trussed ducks and other food offerings), and a glistening pile of overturned chariots. When Carter and Carnar-

von got their senses together again, they realized all at
once that there was no coffin in the room. Was this then
merely a hiding place for treasure? They examined the
room very intently once again, and now they saw that
the two statues stood one on either side of a sealed doorway. Gradually the truth dawned on them. They were
but on the threshold of their discovery. What they saw
was just an antechamber. Behind the guarded door there
would be other rooms, perhaps a whole series of them,
and in one of them, beyond any shadow of doubt they
would find the Pharaoh lying.

But as they thought the thing over, the explorers were

Statues guarding Tut-ankh-Amen's burial chamber
(Courtesy of the Metropolitan Museum of Art by permission of Miss Phyllis Walker)

by no means certain that their first wild expectations would actually come to pass. Perhaps that sealed doorway, like the two before it, had also been re-opened. In that case there was no telling what lay behind it.

On the following day they took down the door through which they had been peeping, and just as soon as the electric connections had been made and they could see things clearly, they rushed over to the doubtful door between the royal sentinels. From a distance it had looked untouched, but when they examined it more closely, they saw that here again the robbers had been before them; near the bottom was distinct evidence that

A portion of the treasure in the tomb of Tut-ankh-Amen
(Courtesy of the Metropolitan Museum of Art by permission of Miss Phyllis Walker)

a small hole had been made and filled up and re-sealed. The robbers had indeed been stopped, but not before they had got into the inner chamber.

It took almost as much self-command not to break down that door and see how much damage the robbers had done as to have filled in the staircase after it had once been cleared. But Carter and Carnarvon were not treasure-seekers; they were archaeologists, and they would not take the chance of injuring the objects within the antechamber just to satisfy their curiosity. For the moment they let that go and turned their attention to the things already before them.

There was enough there to leave them altogether bewildered. But while they were yet going crazily from one object to another and calling excitedly to each other, they stumbled upon yet another discovery. In the wall, hidden behind one of the monstrous couches, was a small, irregular hole, unquestionably made by the plunderers and never re-sealed. They dragged their powerful electric light to the hole and looked in. Another chamber, smaller than the one they were in, but even more crowded with objects! And everything was in the most amazing mess they had ever seen. The cemetery officials had made some attempt to clean up the antechamber after the robbers and to pile up the funeral furniture in some sort of order, but in the annex they had left things just as they were, and the robbers had done their work "about as thoroughly as an earthquake." Not a single inch of floor space remained unlittered.

The back panel of Tut-ankh-Amen's golden throne
(Courtesy of the Metropolitan Museum of Art by permission of Miss Phyllis Walker)

Carter and Carnarvon drew a long breath and sobered down. They realized now that the job before them was going to take months and months. It would be a monumental task to photograph, label, mend, pack and ship all this furniture, clothing, food, these chariots, weapons, walking sticks, jewels—this museumful of treasures.

CHAPTER XVII

In All His Glory

ALL the time they were working, Carter and Carnarvon were, of course, feverishly anxious to know what lay beyond the guarded door. Many a time they glanced at it, but never once did they weaken. Not until every article was safely stowed away and the last bit of dust sifted for a possible bead or bit of inlay did they permit themselves to think of exploring farther.

But at length the day came, and in a hushed stillness—they had invited about twenty people to witness the opening of the door—Carter mounted a platform and with trembling hands very carefully chipped away the plaster and picked out the stones that made up the upper part. Then, when the hole was large enough to look through, he put his electric light on the other side and saw at a distance of a yard from him, and stretching as far as he could see, what appeared to be a wall of solid gold. He removed a few more stones, and then he understood. This was indeed the burial chamber, and the golden wall was an immense gilt shrine built to cover and protect the sarcophagus.

It took two hours to remove the doorway. Carter then let himself down into the burial chamber, which was some four feet below the level of the antechamber, and Lord Carnarvon came on behind through the narrow passage between the shrine and the wall. It was immense, that shrine. It practically filled the room, rising to nine feet and measuring seventeen on the long side and eleven on the short. And from top to bottom it was overlaid with gold.

Carter and Carnarvon did not stop to examine the decorations. At one end of the shrine were great folding doors, and to these they hurried, disregarding everything else. The all-absorbing question was: had the thieves got inside? They drew the bolts, swung back the doors. Inside was a second shrine with bolted doors just as before, and upon the bolts a seal—unbroken. The king was safe. In time they would remove one by one the encasing shrines and before them in full regalia would lie a king of Egypt, unseen by human eyes, untouched by human hands, for three thousand and three hundred years.

With hearts at ease the explorers now moved to examine everything there was to see. They unrolled the wire of their electric light and passed on to the farthest end of the chamber.

To their astonishment, instead of coming to a dead

wall, they saw a low door. It stood open as if inviting them into the room beyond, and passing through, they saw at the first glance that, though smaller than the outer ones, this room contained the greatest treasures of the tomb. Facing the doorway stood a monument so lovely that they gasped with wonder. It was a chest, shaped like a shrine, and overlaid with gold. On the top were sculptured cobras, and about them statues of the four goddesses of the dead, standing with outstretched arms, protecting and guarding the shrine. Directly in front of the entrance stood the emblems of the under-world—the jackal-god, Anubis, lying on a shrine resting on a sled, and behind him the head of a bull on a stand. A great number of black shrines and chests stood on one side of the chamber, all closed save one through the open doors of which the explorers could see statues of Tut-ankh-Amen standing on black leopards. Miniature coffins, model boats and yet another chariot stood in various places about the room, while in the center were a number of caskets of ivory and wood. The thieves had certainly been there, but they could not have taken much because the seals on most of the caskets were still intact.

Carter and Carnarvon felt now as Prince Yuaa's excavators had felt. These were not the relics of a life of three thousand years ago. These were the things of yesterday, of a year or two ago. Tut-ankh-Amen had not reigned in 1400 B. C. He had but just died and they—two Englishmen strangely suspended in time and space—were taking part in the ceremonies of his burial. Not

Statuette of Tut-ankh-Amen on a black leopard
(Courtesy of the Metropolitan Museum of Art by permission of Miss Phyllis Walker)

the unbelievable tomb, but the actual world of the twentieth century seemed unreal to these enchanted explorers.

It was their plan to go on immediately with the work of dismantling the shrines. But for some unfortunate reason the Government now started an argument with the excavators. The work had to be postponed. And while they waited, Lord Carnarvon died.

It was thus with a heavy sense of loss that Carter returned to the tomb to dismantle the shrines—a hard task even for a light heart. The sarcophagus practically filled the chamber, leaving scarcely any room to work in. The sections of the outer shrine, moreover, weighed from a quarter to three-quarters of a ton each. They were almost impossible to handle without injury. And to prove his patience further, Carter found not two but four shrines about the sarcophagus. Eighty days passed before he could get them safely removed.

But at last the sarcophagus stood free, a magnificent chest carved from a single block of yellow quartzite, and sculptured in high relief with goddesses so placed that their outstretched arms and wings encircled the sarcophagus. Strangely enough, the lid of the chest was made not of quartzite but of granite, cracked and patched, though stained to match the quartzite. The workmen, Carter decided, must have dropped the original lid, and there being no time to make another to match, granite had been used instead. That, too, had been cracked in the narrow quarters, and Carter, who had the task of removing the ton and a quarter of stone, understood why the Egyptians had decided to let well enough alone.

In all these many weeks the excavator's emotions had been steadily mounting, for with every day that passed the final mystery drew closer. Even the moment when he had first looked into the antechamber seemed to Carter less dramatic than the one he was looking forward to now as the workmen hauled up the lid of the sarcophagus. In an intense silence it was raised from its bed.

At first sight the contents were disappointing. Linen shrouds swathed whatever lay within and prevented his seeing anything. But when Carter had feverishly pushed back the folds on folds of linen, he saw a coffin of such unsurpassed beauty that he was speechless. It was in the form of the king himself and was decorated for the most part in low relief, but the head and hands were fully sculptured in the round, in massive gold. The hands, crossed over the breast, held the Crook and Flail, the face was wrought in sheet gold, the eyes were of aragonite and obsidian, the eyebrows and eyelids of lapis lazuli glass. Upon the forehead of the boy king in brilliant inlay were worked the Cobra and the Vulture, the symbols of Upper and Lower Egypt, and about these was twined a tiny wreath of flowers, which Carter guessed must have been the farewell offering of the widowed girl queen. "Among all that regal splendor," Carter afterwards said, "there was nothing so beautiful as those few withered flowers, still retaining their tinge of color. They told us what a short period three thousand three hundred years really was—but Yesterday and the Morrow."

To raise the lid of the coffin was the next task. Carter already guessed there would probably be another coffin nested inside. That is what he found. The inner coffin was also in human form, presenting another portrait of

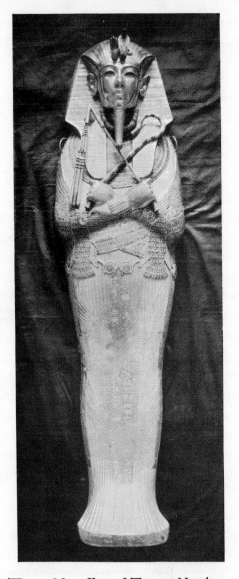

The gold coffin of Tut-ankh-Amen

(Courtesy of the Metropolitan Museum of Art by permission of Miss Phyllis Walker)

the king, and was sumptuously inlaid with colored glass on gold foil. But when the lid of this coffin was raised, there lay within it a third coffin, strangely heavy, and proving to be of solid gold.

The onlookers could not believe their eyes. They had been led to suppose that the funeral glory of the Pharaohs was very great, but so much they had not even dreamed. No wonder the robbers had always managed to find the royal tombs! The value of the gold in the coffin alone was $2,500,000. And Tut-ankh-Amen was but the least of Egypt's kings, a mere boy who ruled in the least glamorous period of Egypt's history. What must have been the funeral trappings of the great Pharaohs in the prime of Egypt's glory!

These were the thoughts that passed through the dazed spectators' minds while they stood awestruck about the innermost coffin of Tut-ankh-Amen. Then the final lid was raised by its golden handles. The mummy of the king lay disclosed. Over the face was a mask of beaten gold—another portrait of the ruler—while about the body was disposed layer after layer of beautiful objects. Beneath the mask was a lovely diadem, about the neck a heap of amulets and necklaces, on the chest breastplates of gold, along the right thigh the Vulture of Upper Egypt, along the left thigh the Uraeus of Lower Egypt, emblems detached from the crown. Over the legs were four collarettes, over the feet were gold sandals, over the toes and fingers gold stalls, about the arms bracelets of gold and silver inlaid with precious

Perfume vase of Tut-ankh-Amen and his queen
(Courtesy of the Metropolitan Museum of Art by permission of Miss Phyllis Walker)

stones. Altogether one-hundred-and-forty-three objects
were disposed about the body in one-hundred-and-one
separate groups!

With trembling fingers Carter examined the treasures. How privileged above all men he had been to do that which others had dreamed of all their lives! Never before had such a find been made. Never had fancy even conjured up such magnificence. What was it worth? Fifteen millions? Twenty? What did the money value matter! Carter knew that as an emblem of a lost civilization, the tomb of Tut-ankh-Amen was priceless. Of all those royal tombs it alone—and only in part—had baffled the greed of man, but it alone would suffice to bring to life the buried world of the Pharaohs, that never-equaled world of glamor and glitter and slavery and toil, of terror and magic and beauty and skill.

PART III

CHAPTER XVIII

Mounds of Mystery

NOT so long ago everybody who came to Egypt, and even all who saw Egypt's monuments at secondhand through books, took it for granted that the Valley of the Nile was the cradle of civilization—that here in the fertile strip along the river the arts had first sprung up. Who could dispute it? What other corner of the earth could possibly lay claim to a civilization that went back so far into the childhood of man?

There was, to be sure, the Tigris-Euphrates Valley. Many traditions clung to it. Legend said that the Land between the Rivers had been the home of a civilization so old that it reached back to a time when men were like gods. They said that in this Mesopotamian plain great cities had stood and kings had reigned whose sway extended far beyond their own dominions. They spoke of priests phenomenally wise, of gardens pre-eminent in beauty, of towers that were the wonder of the world.

And, indeed, the terrifying names of certain kings did hang over the region—Tiglath-pileser, Sennacherib, Nebuchadnezzar. The Hebrew prophets had cried loudly and bitterly against the wickedness of Nineveh and Babylon, the Hebrew records had noted the arrogance and cruelty of the empire builders who had oppressed them, and certainly this was evidence of a sort. Yes, Nineveh and Babylon had been. But where had they gone to? How was it possible for a vast civilization to have lived and died and left no trace behind?

Certainly nothing in the character of the country hinted that here a complex civilization had existed, that here great Babylon had towered and Nineveh "belched forth her all-consuming wrath." In all this dull Mesopotamian plain there was nothing to impress the eye or stir the imagination. There was nothing to suggest that the miserable villagers, the untamed Bedawin and murderous Kurds had had a noble ancestry. Neither pyramids nor temples nor statues nor obelisks proclaimed a vanished glory, and travelers whose eyes were on the lookout for signs of it could find nothing more than a broken brick or two inscribed with signs that none could read. They picked these bricks up on the mounds that rose here and there dully from the plain. When they asked the natives what the mounds were, no one could tell them. They were mounds, that's all. Had they not always been there, in their time, and their fathers' and their fathers' fathers'?

It was an answer that satisfied the Bedawin, and yet

anyone could see that the mounds were not works of nature. What was their secret? They were too large for burial mounds. Was it possible that ruined cities slumbered there?

This was the question that a few people were asking a hundred years ago. Now the secret is out. Hoary Egypt no longer holds sway over antiquity, for a civilization as old or older is fast coming to light. Out of the mounds that rise along the Tigris River and in the Euphrates Valley have sprung ruined palaces and temples. The lost art and history of several thousand years have miraculously come to life. And now that we have them, the wonder is anybody ever asked where they had gone to.

"And it came to pass," says the story of the Tower of Babel, "that they found a plain in the land of Shinar; and they dwelt there. And they said to one another, Come, let us make brick, and burn them thoroughly. And *they had brick for stone*, and slime had they for mortar."

Why, of course! Here, if people had only stopped to think, was the key to the mystery. The Babylonians had to build with brick! Babylonia was a plain made of the sediment brought down by the great rivers. Her tragedy was that she had no stone and that this sediment had to be made into sun-dried brick, which became the traditional building material even in Assyria where stone might have been used. Now crude sun-dried brick is a good enough material so long as it is kept in repair, but if you neglect it, it soon goes to pieces. Even in the merciful climate of Egypt the brick palaces of the Pharaohs crumbled in time. In Babylonia and Assyria the climate was far less kind. An ancient record tells us that forty-five years of neglect were enough to reduce a temple nearly to ruins. Was it surprising, then, that two thousand years should have reduced the defeated cities of Babylonia and Assyria, fired and swamped by the enemy, into ugly, shapeless mounds?

Two thousand years is a long, long time. No wonder that as generation succeeded generation people forgot even the meaning of the mounds. No wonder that they became "mounds, that's all." The real wonder is that with such a clue at hand Europe should have waited so long to solve their mystery.

CHAPTER XIX

Assyria Wakes Up

WHEN in 1842 a Frenchman named Paul Emile Botta received an appointment as consular agent to the city of Mosul in Mesopotamia, the news—if it was published at all—probably appeared in one of the back pages of the Paris papers. Nobody thought it a matter of the least importance. No one had the slightest suspicion that this insignificant consular agent would in a short time startle the world and become a front-page sensation.

It happened, however, that Monsieur Botta was a man of very exceptional character. He was a naturalist who had gone into the consular service in Egypt and had lived in the dangerous climate of Yemen and Syria only so that he might get on with his scientific work. An energetic, practical sort of man, he was, at thirty-seven years of age, still a dreamer. And to be a determined dreamer of dreams was the most important quality he could have had for the project he nursed in his mind.

Long before receiving his appointment to Mosul, Botta, who had a strong interest in history (being the nephew of a celebrated historian), had suspected what might lie in the Mesopotamian mounds. And now no sooner did he find himself on the ground than he prepared to find out how far his suspicions were right. He was no archaeologist; he knew that. Nevertheless, for the labors he had in mind he felt he was not too badly equipped. He was hardened to the climate, he could talk the language of the people and he knew perfectly how to adjust himself to native habits. Moreover, he had scientific training; and wasn't a scientific approach to a problem half the battle?

With faith and hope high, therefore, and the scientific spirit uppermost, he set out first of all to examine the whole region around Mosul. He would go into one house after another and ask the people whether they had anything which was very old. If they brought out some antiquity, he would immediately buy it and try to trace it to the place where it had originally come from. All this he undertook for the sake of choosing a likely site to excavate. But it all led nowhere, and in the end he had to decide to dig at random in any mound at all. Kouyunjik lay directly across from Mosul. He might just as well dig there as anywhere.

So, with none of his ardor abated, he began to excavate. But when a solid year of work had given him nothing more to show for it than a few inscribed bricks and some fragments of sculpture, Botta's enthusiasm began to wear thin. He was beginning to question his own convictions. Could it be that he was on the wrong track after all? Was it possible that the relics he dreamed of finding in this mound existed only in his imagination? Then one day as he was gloomily surveying the digging, an Arab stepped up to him. It was not a local Arab but one who had chanced by from a neighboring village and had stopped to see what was going on. He addressed Botta respectfully. Was the Frank looking for inscribed bricks? Then why did he dig in so unprofitable a place? In his own village of Khorsabad there were plenty of bricks. He would get the Frank as many as he desired. He himself was a dyer. He built his ovens of just such bricks.

Botta merely brushed the man aside. He had had such unfortunate experiences with Arabs that he didn't believe one of them could tell the truth if he tried. Even when the persistent dyer had brought him two inscribed bricks from his village, Botta stood firm. And yet the man's words stuck in his mind. As time went by and nothing came of his effort, he began to weaken. After all, was there any harm in sending a few men to see?

He had not long to wait. Less than a week later an excited messenger, bursting with his news, brought word that two parallel walls covered with inscriptions and sculptures had been dug up. Botta listened in stupefaction. Was it possible? So quickly? He didn't dare let himself believe. Not until his personal servant had rid-

Assyrian sculpture showing spoil being taken from a city

den down and back and brought actual proof of the find would the long disappointed excavator let his feelings go. But then there was no controlling them. He rushed off at once to the scene of action and by the time he had entered the trench was in a delirium of joy.

Here were the walls he had dreamed of for so long. But what exactly did they mean? What had he dug up? He didn't know. The people who looked at him out of the sculptures were all new to him. Never before had he seen such clothing, weapons, objects. It was a page of history he had never read. But one clue to this ancient people was before him—the wedge-shaped writing that appeared between the sculptures. Botta could not read what it said, but the fact that it was there at all was significant. Cuneiform writing had ceased to be used after Alexander conquered the world. It was clear that the sculptured people had lived before the conquest. These walls were not, perhaps, the walls of Nineveh; but Botta could scarcely doubt that they had been built by Assyrians.

His head teeming with conjectures, he sat right down in the midst of his workmen and began to sketch the most important reliefs and inscriptions. He could spare only one day from his consular duties at this time. But he didn't need more than one day to make up his mind that this was where he was going to dig from now on. Immediately all the men were transferred to the new site and with renewed vigor the work went forward.

Wall followed wall. Khorsabad was even more prom-

Assyrian sculpture showing soldiers escaping by swimming on inflated bladders

ising than Botta had dared to hope. A seemingly endless succession of rooms filled with relics of the past was rising from the mound. Here was the sculptured assault of a fortress, here scribes recorded the heads of the slain, here captives were being led away or else cruelly impaled, here were chariots, spirited horses, here were conquerors wearing along with their regal robes an air of satisfied superiority. Botta was convinced that his highest hopes had been realized and that he had indeed unearthed a palace of the Assyrian kings. Yet he wrote home very guardedly. "I believe myself to be the first," he said, "who has discovered sculptures which with some reason can be referred to the period when Nineveh was flourishing."

When he wrote this, he expected there would be a stir at home. He had no notion there would be such a to-do as there was. The French people entered into the plan of excavation with the wildest enthusiasm. Such marvelous work should have every assistance, they declared. Money must be raised at once to help Botta continue. An artist must be sent out to sketch everything that could not be taken to France.

But while he waited for help to reach him, Botta was finding himself in a world of difficulties. The sculptures he had dug up with such effort would not stand when exposed to the air. If he set up props of wood to hold up the walls, the natives who lived in the village on top of the mound plundered them as soon as his back was turned. The Pasha of Mosul also became extremely hostile. Certain that Botta was digging for gold, he put every obstacle in his way. Now he would throw the diggers into prison and try to torture a confession out of them. Now he would appoint watchmen to hang around in order to seize every piece of gold as it appeared. Then, again, he would write to Constantinople to say that Botta was digging trenches on the mound with the intent of putting up a fortress. His designs failing, he would for one reason or another prohibit the work. Then he would let Botta continue but at the same time would secretly forbid the villagers to sell him their houses. To keep going under these conditions, to direct, to rescue, to sketch, to make notes was a task that only the tireless energy of such a man as Botta could accomplish. The rescue of Assyria was a triumph of character more than of skill.

For us, whose history books have always been illustrated with pictures of Assyrians and their winged bulls and lion hunts and battle scenes, it is hard to appreciate the excitement that took place when three years later Botta's sculptures and bas-reliefs from Dur-Sharrukin (Sargon-Burg) finally arrived at Havre. To understand it we have to stop and think that no one in Europe had at that time yet seen anything of the kind. Assyria had been asleep for two thousand years. Up to the year 1842 a single case not three feet square had held all that there was of Nineveh and Babylon. And now here was the art of the people before whom the nations of Asia had trembled. Here were those wolves of the past them-

Mede bringing two horses as tribute to King Sargon
(Courtesy of the Metropolitan Museum of Art)

selves. This is what they had looked like. This is how
they had besieged cities, scaled walls, given battle, impaled inhabitants, carried away captives and spoil. It
was not so much the high artistic quality of the sculptures that kept people staring hours at a time. It was the
thrill they got in seeing for the first time this mysterious
people whose name through the ages had come to sig-
nify cruelty and arrogant power.

King Sargon and the sculptures from his palace in
Dur-Sharrukin received an ovation such as they had
never had in their own time. Artists, writers, historians
seized on Botta's treasures with joy. No longer would
they have to rely entirely on their imagination. Here at
last were real costumes, real weapons, real chariots, real

Assyrians to work with. And all this was only a beginning. Now that Botta had begun to excavate, others
would go into the field. The whole forgotten civilization
would yet be theirs.

They were entirely right. Already Austen Henry Layard, who was to become one of the world's luckiest archaeologists, had his eye on the mounds.

CHAPTER XX

Layard Prepares to Dig

LAYARD was an Englishman for whom the "East" had always been a magic word. As a youngster the *Arabian Nights* had set him on fire with desire to see Aleppo, Damascus, Baghdad, Isfahan, and from then on he had in all seriousness prepared himself for Eastern travel. He read everything he could about it. He learned the Arabic characters and a little of the Persian language. He got lessons in the use of the sextant from a retired sea captain. He provided himself with telescope, thermometers, barometer, compass, watch. He even got a medical friend to instruct him in the symptoms of the diseases he would be most likely to meet with in the East, and in the use of the lancet for the treatment of wounds—all of which knowledge was of inestimable value to him later.

Such instruction seemed to be the only kind he could digest. Law, which at the age of sixteen he was set down to study, made him utterly miserable. After six years in a London solicitor's office he felt he must either break loose or break his heart, and, deciding the first was preferable, he set off alone on a tour through Sweden and Russia—and then on to the East.

He was young, very handsome, strong, intelligent, daring. The world opened its heart to him, and he opened his eyes and his mind and drank everything in. No place was too out of the way for him because he didn't have to get anywhere; no people too uncivilized because he wasn't afraid of roughing it; no experience too dangerous because he had plenty of courage. He sought shelter in the tents of wild tribesmen as confidently as the ordinary traveler seeks a room in a hotel, and if now and again he was robbed, he felt it was just a part of seeing the world of men and things.

Everything interested him. And yet nothing quite so stirred his imagination as the great ruins of the past. When in 1840 his travels at last brought him to the Assyrian mounds, a strange fascination took hold of him. Nothing he had seen before had affected him so deeply. "Those huge mounds of Assyria," he wrote afterwards, "made a deeper impression upon me, gave rise to more serious thought and more earnest reflection than the temples of Baalbec or the theatres of Ionia." And when two years later Layard met Botta at Mosul and talked with him, the desire to explore the mounds crystallized into determination.

But he had no money. For the time being he was

forced to turn away. However, he could think and talk of nothing but mounds and Assyria, excavations and antiquities, from morning to night, until in the end his enthusiasm so infected the British Ambassador that Sir Stratford Canning made him a present of £60 with which to begin work. It was 1845, five years since Layard had first started to dream of excavating the mounds. He did not lose an instant. To the £60 he immediately added his own small savings, and with the lightest heart in the world, with no servant and no baggage except a pair of saddlebags, he set out to resurrect Nineveh. He knew that his funds were ridiculously small for the task he meant to undertake. But he felt sure that if he met with the good fortune he expected, money for excavation would flow in. He rode night and day to get to Mosul.

Now Layard was prepared to endure all sorts of hardships and to meet all sorts of obstacles, but he hardly expected to meet the sort of thing which the worthy Governor of Mosul was to put in his path. Whether this was the same gentleman who had made life miserable for Botta, Layard does not say in the record of his adventures, but apparently he was a man of the same pattern. He was a Turk—the territory was all under Turkish rule—but he looked much less like a Turk or a Chinaman or a Hottentot than he did like an ogre. He had one eye, one ear, was short, fat, deeply marked with the smallpox, and was blessed with a harsh voice and uncouth gestures. As for his character, that accorded very well with his appearance.

"Nature," wrote Layard about him afterwards, "had placed hypocrisy beyond his reach." He could not pretend to be anything but what he was, a rascal through and through. When he had first been sent out from Constantinople to govern the country, he had begun by charging the natives "tooth-money," a tax that was to compensate him, he said, for the wear and tear on his teeth when chewing the coarse food of the villagers. But this act of statesmanship was only a mild preamble. When his administration really got started, the whole population was reduced to a state of terror and despair. He plundered the villagers and he plundered the townsfolk and he chopped heads right and he chopped heads left. With the one exception that he did not eat little children, he lived up to the popular conception of an ogre.

The people, Layard soon learned, were entirely at his mercy. One day, taking sudden hope because a traveler from the outside world was among them, the townsfolk began to whisper that the hated Pasha was about to be deposed. As always happens in such cases, the whisper reached the ears of the governor. He rose to the occasion. He pretended to be suddenly taken ill and was carried almost lifeless to his palace. When on the following day the palace was closed, the people naturally thought he was dead. They burst into rejoicings. Allah had intervened for them! And then suddenly in the midst of their rejoicings the Pasha appeared on the scene as well as ever and immediately proceeded to strip of their possessions all those who had as yet escaped his greed. They had "spread reports detrimental to his authority," he declared.

When Layard saw that this was the sort of person with whom he had to deal, he did not dare to reveal his plans about excavating. He procured guns and spears, and saying that he was going to hunt boars in a neighboring village, quietly set off down the Tigris River.

The country was in an uproar. The roads were infested with ferocious Bedawin, who, since they could not revenge themselves on the Pasha for robbing them, vowed they would get back at anybody who came their way. The outlook for excavating was not very bright. But Layard had so much personal charm and such a remarkable gift for making friends with the natives that before night he had won the firm affection of Awad, chief of the tribe that was encamped nearest the mound called Nimroud, and by morning he had six workmen on the spot.

He was in a fever to begin. He had spent the whole night seeing visions of palaces underground, gigantic monsters, sculptured figures, endless inscriptions. Now his long-cherished hopes were to be either realized or dashed. But it needed only one glance at the mound to see that he had made no mistake at all in choosing the site. The whole surface was covered with fragments of inscribed bricks. He stood there spellbound, not able to make up his mind where to begin operations, when

Awad led him to a piece of alabaster which appeared above the soil. That settled the problem. Layard started the digging right there, and such was his good fortune that a few hours' work revealed the upper edges of several adjoining slabs. It was evident that this was the wall of a chamber.

He was delighted, but not yet satisfied. He left half the workmen to continue on the spot and led the rest to another corner of the mound where he had observed fragments of alabaster. And again his luck held. Almost immediately he came upon a wall bearing inscriptions, and by night time Layard had good evidence that "buildings of considerable extent existed in the mound." Now he could sleep in peace. He had done one day's work with six men and had disclosed the whereabouts of two palaces!

CHAPTER XXI

Bulls, Lions and Difficulties

ON the following day five more workmen presented themselves. In their eyes the foreigner was certainly a madman to go grubbing in the mounds. But he paid regular wages and if he foolishly wanted to go on spending his good money for stones, they were perfectly willing to look for them. Awad, the chief of the tribe, however, had his own ideas as to what the excavator was after, and one day when Layard came upon some ivory figures showing traces of gilding and some bits of gold leaf, the Arab's suspicions were confirmed. He called Layard confidentially aside and produced some scraps of gold leaf wrapped in a piece of dingy paper. "O Bey," he said, "Wallah! your books are right, and the Franks know that which is hid from the true believer. Here is the gold sure enough, and please God, we shall find it all in a few days. Only don't say anything about it to those Arabs, for they are asses and cannot hold their tongues.

The matter will come to the ears of the Pasha."

In course of time it did. That worthy was already aware of what Layard was doing at Nimroud, and the excavator had not been long at work when spies in the form of a captain and some soldiers were sent down to keep an eye on everything he was doing. The matter of the gold leaf had no sooner come to light than the captain briefly informed the excavator that he would have to stop.

Layard made speed at once to get to Mosul and find out the reason why. And now he got the full flavor of the Pasha's rich personality. The governor was full of apologies. He deeply regretted it, but the mound had been used as a Mohammedan burial ground and it was forbidden by law to disturb a tomb. The natives would be enraged, he said. "No, I cannot allow you to proceed; you are my dearest and most intimate friend; if anything happens to you, what grief should I not suffer!"

After this profession of friendship, imagine Layard's amazement when the captain, whom he had managed to convert into a friend, privately informed him that at the Pasha's command he and his troops had been spending two nights bringing gravestones from distant villages and making graves on the mound! "We have destroyed more real tombs of the true believers," said the captain, "in making sham ones, than you could have defiled between the Zab and Selamiyah. We have killed our horses and ourselves in carrying those accursed stones."

Fortunately for Layard, the mills of the gods had just

about got around to grinding up the worthy Pasha. In another month his excellency was in very sad straits. His governorship had been taken from him and he sat miserably in a dilapidated room through the roof of which the rain poured down on him. "Thus it is with God's creatures," he said to Layard, who had come to see him. "Yesterday all these dogs were kissing my feet; today everyone and everything falls upon me, even the rain!"

With the Pasha removed, Layard could breathe freely, and soon great things were on the way. One morning as the excavator was approaching the mound, he saw two Arabs riding toward him at top speed. "Hasten, O Bey," one of them cried, "hasten to the diggers, for they have found Nimrod himself. Allah, it is wonderful, but it is true! we have seen him with our eyes. There is no God but God!"

Now Layard, of course, knew that the Arabs thought the mound to be the burial place of Nimrod, that "mighty hunter before the Lord" of whom the Bible speaks. But he was not in the least deceived by what the messenger said. He knew what it was they had found, for his dearest hope all through the digging had been to come upon such colossal winged statues as Botta had unearthed at Khorsabad. In great excitement he hurried to the mound, and even as he had hoped, so it was. The upper part of a figure was rising from the earth. No wonder the Arabs had been terrified by the sight. "It required no stretch of the imagination," Layard said later, "to conjure up the most strange fancies. This gigantic head, blanched with age, thus rising from the bowels of the earth, might well have belonged to one of those fearful beings which are pictured in the traditions of the country, as appearing to mortals, slowly ascending from the regions below."

There was such excitement as the neighborhood had not seen for many a year. The Sheikh from the encampment arrived post haste on the scene with half his tribe behind him, but it was some time before he could be prevailed upon to go down into the pit and see for himself that the image was only stone. "This is not the work of men's hands," he declared when he had finally got up his courage to investigate, "but of those infidel giants of whom the Prophet, peace be with him! has said that they were higher than the tallest date tree; this is one of the idols which Noah, peace be with him! cursed before the flood." And all the bystanders agreed with him.

By-and-by the news got to Mosul and there was more commotion. The Cadi had no distinct notion about what had been uncovered. Was it the bones of the mighty hunter or only his image? he wanted to know. Nor did the Pasha very clearly remember whether Nimrod was a true-believing prophet or an infidel. But anyhow they were going to do something about it before the wrath of Allah descended upon them. Layard consequently received word to treat the remains with respect and stop the excavations right away. It was not until the Cadi and the Pasha had been satisfied that no harm was being

Winged lion which once guarded the palace gate of Ashurnasirpal (Courtesy of the Metropolitan Museum of Art)

done to any pious ancestor of the true believers that the work could go on again.

The colossal statue was only the first of many. As the excavation progressed, no fewer than thirteen pairs of winged lions and bulls came forth from this, the palace of Ashurnasirpal in the ancient city of Calah. But never again did the Arabs become quite so excited as that first time. Only when the winged lion was finally being taken away to be shipped to England did they again rise to the occasion. They drew the resurrected beast along in procession and all the natives followed with music and dancing and shouting and spear-tossing, while the Sheikh voiced his wonder and admiration to Layard.

"I have lived on these lands for years," he said. "My father and the father of my father pitched their tents here before me; but they never heard of these figures. For twelve hundred years have the true believers (and, praise be to God! all true wisdom is with them alone) been settled in this country and none of them ever heard of a palace under ground. Neither did they who went before them. But lo! here comes a Frank from many days' journey off, and he walks up to the very place, and he takes a stick and makes a line here and makes a line there. Here, says he, is the palace; there, says he, is the gate; and he shows us what has been all our lives beneath our feet, without our having known anything about it. Wonderful, wonderful! Is it by books, is it by magic, is it by your prophets, that you have learnt these things? Speak, O Bey; tell me the secret of wisdom."

But Layard did not answer. He himself had been thinking along the same lines. He himself had been marveling that far-distant and comparatively new nations should have kept the frail record of the Assyrians and should be able to teach their descendants, or those who had taken their places, where their cities and monuments had once stood.

CHAPTER XXII

In the Bosom of Kuyunjik

LAYARD had heard from Botta all about his fruitless year of digging on the mound called Kuyunjik; nevertheless, now that the Ogre of Mosul was no longer around to spy upon him, the excavator decided to see what he could do there. He felt it was impossible for so large a mound to be without relics, and with the greatest care examined the whole surface and chose his ground. If he had been gifted with the power of seeing through the earth, he could not have chosen better.

Profiting by his experience at Nimroud, Layard began by digging down to the platform of sun-dried brick on which he now knew the Assyrians used to put up their large buildings. About twenty feet down he reached it and then went on to make trenches in various directions. The results were almost immediate. His workmen one morning came on a wall, and following it along, arrived at an entrance formed by winged bulls and leading into a hall. After four weeks' labor, nine long narrow chambers stood revealed. Many of the sculptures had been reduced to lime because the palace had been burned, but enough remained to show Layard that all he had found in Nimroud would be as nothing compared with what he would dig up here. For this patience-trying Kuyunjik, which Botta had vainly explored so long and in the end abandoned, was nothing less than Nineveh, the great Assyrian stronghold, and these walls the walls of the palace of Sennacherib. Now the terror of the nations would no longer be just a name. Now the dread king whose pestilence-stricken armies had melted overnight before Jerusalem would be something more than tradition. This was real. This was history. Here was the palace, here his pictured deeds, here the very cylinders of clay on which he had caused his cruel deeds to be inscribed.

Sennacherib, the great king,
the mighty king, king of the universe, king of Assyria,
king of the four quarters of the earth; the wise ruler,
favorite of the great gods, guardian of the right,
lover of justice; who lends support,
who comes to the aid of the needy, who turns his
  thoughts to pious deeds;
perfect hero, mighty man;
first among all princes, the powerful one who con-
  sumes
the insubmissive, who strikes the wicked with the

thunderbolt;
the God Assur, the great mountain, an unrivaled king-
*   ship*
has entrusted to me, and above all those
who dwell in palaces, has made powerful my weapons;
from the upper sea of the setting sun
to the lower sea of the rising sun,
all humankind he has brought in submission at my
*   feet,*
and mighty kings feared my warfare
leaving their abodes and
flying alone, like the sudinnu, the bird of the cliffs,
to some inaccessible place.

In this way Sennacherib began. This was the gentle
preamble to how he had plundered, made captive,
burned, slain, impaled and so brought "humankind" in
submission to his feet. The lightest mood Sennacherib
ever seems to have assumed is "I besieged, I conquered,
I despoiled, I devastated, I burned with fire." As the
scholars went on reading how he had plunged his steeds
into his enemies' blood as into a river and filled the plain
with the bodies of their warriors like grass, the best
thing they could find to say of Sennacherib was that he
had not been so bad as some of the Assyrian kings—
Ashurnasirpal, say.

Two hundred and sixty of their fighting men I put to
the sword, and I cut off their heads and I piled them in

*heaps. . . . I built a pillar over against his city gate, and
I flayed all the chief men who had revolted, and I covered
the pillar with their skins; some I walled up within the
pillar, and some upon the pillar on stakes I impaled, and
others I fixed to stakes round about the pillar. . . . Three
thousand captives I burned with fire. . . . Their young
men and maidens I burned in the fire.*

This was Ashurnasirpal speaking. But all the kings'
records told the same tale of blood, fire, corpses, torture,
mutilation. As the records piled up, nobody could
longer doubt that the Assyrians had earned their reputation. The Prophet Nahum, living as an exile not far
from Nineveh, had been justified in exclaiming glee-
fully when at last the city began to totter, "For thy hurt
is no healing, thy wounds are all mortal, all that hear of
thy fate smite their hands in rejoicing, for on whom hath
not thy iniquity fallen?"

The Assyrians had ruled the nations by terror. They
had kept their empire going by making the price of in-
submission the most cruel torture men could devise.
And yet, such is human nature that the system worked
in a vicious circle. Oppression was so hard to bear that
subject kings took their chances and revolted, after
which the Assyrians had no choice but to invent new
and worse terrors, which in turn would provoke fresh
rebellions.

The whole history of Assyria as it was pieced together
out of the records was so ugly that it was something of a

relief to Layard to discover that even the cruel Assyrian rulers had not been able to live by blood alone. The heartless Ashurbanipal had actually been fond of books. He had liked them so well that he had caused thirty thousand of them to be collected for his private library. In two rooms built on at a later time to Sennacherib's palace Layard came upon half of the royal hoard.

He did not need to be told as he surveyed the piles of precious tablets that this find was the brightest jewel in his archaeological crown. Anyone could see that. The library was the most revealing thing he could have found. It was a direct route to the mind of the Assyrian people.

King Sennacherib's cavalry in the mountains

(Courtesy of the Metropolitan Museum of Art)

What had they who lived by the sword considered important enough to set down so laboriously in clay? Strangely enough, not their own thoughts. The greatest number of Ashurbanipal's books had been copied from the tablets in the libraries at Babylon and Borsippa and were predominantly of a religious nature—hymns, prayers and so on. Some dealt with omens, dreams and ways of foretelling the future by examining the livers of sacrificial sheep. Many, again, dealt with a darker sort of religion—black magic—and were concerned with charms, incantations and methods of casting out devils. Holy water and the number seven were held to be very good, and magical threads bound seven times around the limbs with "sentences from a holy book" would send any devil packing.

The Assyrians seem to have been fascinated by the study of magic. Yet the library was by no means one-sided. It contained treatises on mathematics and astronomy, letters and public papers, medical works (which again verged on magic), lists of kings, historical notes and even story books. The best of these last, however, it did not fall to Layard's lot to discover. Some time after he had retired from Kuyunjik, where he had covered himself with such glory, Hormuzd Rassam dug up in Ashurbanipal's own palace the other half of the library. It was among these tablets that the great literary creation of the Babylonians was discovered in a way romantic enough to fit in with the thousand thrills of Kuyunjik.

The tablets had been sent to London and placed in the British Museum, where a certain George Smith, an assistant in the Department of Assyrian Antiquities, began to work over them. One day in the fall of 1872, as he was puzzling over a large fragment, the story he read sounded strangely familiar to his mind. It was the story of a great flood. Smith went on puzzling it out, and he now saw that the composition was very much like the Hebrew story of Noah and the Ark. But there was a striking difference. Whereas in the Hebrew version the story of Noah and the Ark stands all alone, the story in the tablet seemed to be a part of a larger composition which told a number of adventures that had happened to a certain Babylonian hero, named Gilgamesh, when he went out in search of eternal life. Naturally Smith was very much excited by his discovery. But where was the rest of the story? It was certainly not in the British Museum. It must still be somewhere in Kuyunjik!

When Smith announced his discovery, the London *Daily Telegraph* promptly came to the rescue. If the scholar would go to Kuyunjik and look for the missing tablets, the paper would advance the sum of one thousand guineas to finance the expedition. The chance of succeeding seemed about as good as finding a needle in a haystack. But George Smith was an enthusiastic young man; he unhesitatingly agreed to go and look for it. And the miracle actually happened. Smith actually did find nearly the whole of the missing portion of the Deluge story upon which the Bible story had been patterned.

CHAPTER XXIII

Working Out a Puzzle

TWO men in a few decades had roused Assyria from a sleep of twenty centuries. Botta had done much, Layard had done much more. But Assyria would never have come into her own had it not been for the geniuses who deciphered the wedge-shaped script symbol by symbol. There is no miracle story more amazing than theirs. Without anything that corresponded to a Rosetta Stone, they worked out the sound and meaning of the wedges in three different languages and even laid down a theory of their origin that has had the most sensational proof.

Ever since the seventeenth century when the Italian traveler Pietra della Valle sent home a copy of a few cuneiform characters and stated his reasons why they ought to be read from left to right, people had puzzled over the wedge-shaped writing. At first a number of scholars were of the opinion that it was not writing at all. It was just a form of decoration, they said, similar to the scrollwork of the Greeks. As time went on, however, and more and more travelers visited the famous ruins at Persepolis and saw the inscriptions on the rocks and monuments there, it became certain that the wedges really were some unknown sort of writing.

This Persepolis was believed—because of the name, Persian City—to be the ancient capital of the nation that conquered the Assyrians. It was natural to think, therefore, that some at least of the wedge-shaped writing—of which there seemed to be three different kinds—was Persian. The question was which was which. In some of the inscriptions the writings appeared side by side in three columns. Was it not likely that the conquerors had put their language in the middle section because it was the most prominent? And was it not likely that the writing in the sections on either side was that of two conquered peoples? Scholars became convinced that this was so. For convenience they called the writing in the center section Class I, and the others Class II and Class III.

The next step towards solving the puzzle was the last easy one anyone could take. A certain scholar picked out a particular wedge that appeared over and over again in the inscriptions of Class I and declared it to be a word separator. And there for a while progress stopped.

The problem of the Rosetta Stone was simple in comparison. There one of the three writings was Greek, which scholars knew very well. But how was it here?

All three languages were just as much of a mystery. No one had the slightest idea what any of the inscriptions were about or what was the meaning or sound of a single one of all those thousands of wedges that looked like nothing so much as bird tracks on wet sand. There seemed to be absolutely nothing to start from. "The problem is insoluble," people said. "It's as hopeless as trying to square the circle or to find the North Pole."

But at last a German scholar, Georg Friedrich Grotefend, a teacher of Greek in the gymnasium at Göttingen, got an inspiration. Eastern peoples, he reasoned, do not readily abandon the ways of their ancestors. If their fathers have done a thing in a certain way, that is the way they do it, too. Take the Egyptian Pharaohs. For 1500 years they built their tombs in the same pyramid form. Now why should not the same thing be true about inscriptions? Maybe the Persian kings wrote their inscriptions in the same form as the kings before them.

He knew that in later years when the Persians had already stopped using cuneiform, they all began their inscriptions in a set form that went like this:

N, great king, king of kings, king of Iran and Aniran, son of N, great king, king of kings, king of Iran and Aniran. . . .

Perhaps, Grotefend reasoned, at the time when the Persian kings yet wrote in cuneiform they used the same form. Perhaps what these Persepolis inscriptions said was this:

*So and so, great king, king of kings, king of This and
That, son of So and so, great king, king of kings, king of
This and That, did something or other.*

If that really was the case, then he had something to begin on. The first word would certainly be the name of a
king, then would come the word separator, and after
that two words, one of which would be *king*. And this
word *king* would be repeated many times in the first
part of the inscription.

Grotefend now examined the inscriptions with this in
mind and what was his joy to find exactly what he had
hoped might be there. In the first part of the inscription
a certain word, which he assumed to be *king,* was repeated over and over again.

Now all the inscriptions at Persepolis, no matter on
what monument, began with one of two words. If these
were, as he thought, really names, then the meaning was
clear: all the monuments had been set up by only two
kings. But on some of the monuments *both* names appeared! That meant, Grotefend decided, that one king
had been the son of the other. He called one king X and
the other king Y. And now the two short inscriptions on
which he was working read as follows:

X king . . . son of Z. . . .
Y king . . . son of X king. . . .

Of course, the thing that at once struck Grotefend
was that the grandfather, Z, did not have the word *king*
after his name, whereas X (the father) and Y (the son)

both did. It was easy to jump to the conclusion: the grandfather had not been a king. But who were the three? Hot on the trail, our scholar began to search through the known Greek records of Persian history for such a group—grandfather not a king, father and son kings. To his dismay he found three such groups, but various reasons soon led him to believe that the particular group he was in search of were Hystaspes, Darius and Xerxes. This was the key other scholars needed. They picked up the work at this point and before long had worked out a number of signs in Class I.

In the meantime, by the most remarkable coincidence, a young army officer, who had not the slightest knowledge of what the scholars were doing, was learning to read cuneiform entirely by his own efforts.

To look at Henry Rawlinson in the year 1827 when the handsome, seventeen-year-old cadet boarded ship for India, nobody would have thought that he had in him the makings of a scholar. Certainly he did not suspect it himself. He had in no way distinguished himself at school. If, as he stood on the deck of his ship, his thoughts went back to his brief academic career, probably the thing that stood out most clearly in his mind was the time he had dressed up as a ghost and frightened a girls' school. But as a matter of fact Rawlinson was so active a lad, so full of fun and ideas that his thoughts were actually very little on the past and very much on the here and now. Already he had thought up a scheme for the amusement of the passengers. He would edit a handwritten weekly newspaper to help pass the tedious four months' journey around the Horn.

Curiously, it was this small bit of amusement that proved to be Rawlinson's first step on the road to becoming the greatest Orientalist of his day. It happened that on board the same ship was the Governor of Bombay, Sir John Malcolm, a distinguished soldier and Oriental scholar. He became interested in the young editor, spent hours talking to him about the Persian language, Persian literature and Persian history, and got Rawlinson so interested in them that at the first opportunity the lad took up the study of Persian. Six years later it was his knowledge of the language that landed him in Persia, less than twenty miles from the great inscription at Behistun.

The region in which he found himself was very rich in antiquities. Cuneiform inscriptions were all around, and Rawlinson hadn't been in Persia a month before he was deep in the study of the wedge-shaped script. He had never heard of Grotefend. He knew nothing about the German's method. And yet his general approach was almost the same; he, too, began by working out names. And, curiously enough, the first names he worked out were Darius, Xerxes, and Hystaspes. His clue was the fact that two of the inscriptions were exactly alike except for three groups, and these he guessed to be names in a father-son relationship.

Rawlinson saw, however, that to master the puzzle he needed a long inscription with lots of names in it. Was not the trilingual inscription at Behistun the very thing? It was very difficult to get at, of course. The king who had caused the writing to be carved—Darius, Rawlinson afterward learned—had taken great ¯care that no later monarch should obliterate his work. He had had the sculptures and writing placed at a sheer height of 300 feet on the face of a bare, living rock that rose 1700 feet into the air. It would take some climbing to get up to it. But was he, said Rawlinson to himself, horseman and hunter and athlete for nothing?

So three or four times a day he would climb the slippery precipice and copy away until he had secured the whole of the Persian part of the inscription. The Babylonian section was impossible to get at without immensely long ladders and plenty of rope and pegs. He came back several years later and at the risk of breaking his neck copied that. But for the present he was content to study the Persian part. For three years he slaved at it, and then in 1846 the Royal Asiatic Society published his translation of what King Darius had told the world about his campaigns. Never was there such a turmoil. People could not believe that anyone had actually performed all alone a feat which was, and must always be, "one of the supreme achievements of the human brain."

Meantime neither Rawlinson nor other scholars had been standing still. While Rawlinson worked on the Class III inscription at Behistun, they had attacked the inscriptions of the same class which Botta and Layard had dug up and which they now knew were Babylonian-

Assyrian. It was a task infinitely harder than deciphering the Persian. Whereas in the ancient Persian every sign stood for a letter, in the Assyrian a sign sometimes stood for a syllable and sometimes for an entire word. Moreover, a sign very seldom represented just *one* syllable or just *one* word. Most of the signs had more than one sound or stood for several different words.

It was all so confusing that the scholars might have got very little except headache out of it had not the library of Ashurbanipal come to their rescue. When the clay tablets were sorted out, it was found that a large group of them contained lists of signs arranged in columns. These lists were nothing less than dictionaries, made for the use of scribes, and these dictionaries contained the very information the scholars were groping for. The lists were sometimes like this:

The meaning, of course, was clear, and the scholars did not hesitate to translate thus:

The sign ⊨⍦ has the syllabic value of li-ib

The sign ⊨⍦ has the syllabic value of da-an

The sign ⊨⍦ has the syllabic value of ka-al

"But how is it possible for so crazy a writing to exist?" people asked when they heard about these amazing lists. "How can anyone read a language in which the selfsame sign stands for three entirely different things? Are those scholars having a joke at our expense?"

The scholars vigorously denied it. "There *is* such a language, and we *can* read it," they said. And one of them suggested a test. "Give us a piece of writing we have never seen before," he said, "and let each of us make a translation independently. Then you can compare the translations and see whether we have all read the same thing or not."

The Royal Asiatic Society took him at his word. They gave a piece of Assyrian-Babylonian writing that had never yet been deciphered to four different scholars, one of them being Rawlinson. Each one independently translated it and sent in his version. And all four translations were alike!

There was such a writing. It could be read. But how did it ever come to be? Why in the world should the Babylonians have invented a system in which one sign meant several such different things?

The scholars were just as puzzled by it as the people who only listened to what the scholars said. But they were certain there must be a reason. They had not hit upon it because they had not dug down far enough. If they would go to the very origin of cuneiform writing, they would find out why. And so they began looking for a clue.

CHAPTER XXIV

A Prophecy Comes True

THE thing that started the scholars off in the right direction was the fact that a single sign sometimes stood for a whole word. That could mean only one thing: the wedges had once been hieroglyphics, and before that pictures. And, indeed, some of the signs looked unmistakably like crude drawings. A sign like this 𐎹, for example, stood for the word *hand*. But what language were the original pictures supposed to represent?

Someone now came forth with a startling new idea. The Babylonians had not invented their writing. The original pictures had represented the writing of an entirely different people, a people who did not even belong to the great Semitic family to which the Hebrews, the Arabs, Phoenicians, Babylonians and Assyrians belonged. The Babylonians and Assyrians had borrowed the writing of this unknown people. And when they took it over, they did two things. First they used the pictures to write the corresponding words in their own language, and then they used the pictures as syllables to write other words in their own language.

This new idea appealed to the scholars tremendously for the reason that it covered all the facts. But people in general were not at all impressed by it. "Just because you can't explain why one sign stands for several sounds, you go and *invent* a people," they scoffed. "If your theory is right, why are there no inscriptions in the original language? Who were these people? Where did they come from? You've got to show us something better than theories before we'll swallow a people nobody has ever even heard of."

But the scholars stood stubbornly by their theory. They even gave a name to the unknown people. *Sumerians* they called them, because on some very old inscriptions the kings of that part of the world had styled themselves "King of Sumer and Akkad." "We'll yet find monuments with inscriptions in the Sumerian language," the scholars said. "The place to look for them is in Babylonia because that is where the oldest inscriptions are coming from."

And before long their prophecy was fulfilled. A French consular agent, digging in the mound of Tellô, brought to light the very thing the scholars had foretold.

Ernest de Sarzec, like Botta and Layard, was a man cut out for Mesopotamian archaeology—he understood life in the desert, he was familiar with Oriental manners and he was physically very fit. Like Botta and Layard, too, he had an enthusiasm for the ancient civilization of the country. There was nothing to do in the dull post to which he had been sent except go hunting; so it was the most natural thing in the world that after two months he should have started digging.

The mounds of Tellô had been suggested to him by a friendly resident of Basra. As described, they hadn't sounded alluring. The mounds, he was told, formed an irregular sort of oval about two-and-a-half miles long by one-and-a-quarter broad, lying eight miles from the nearest town and situated in a district that was a desert half the year and a swamp the other. When with some-what dampened spirits de Sarzec had ridden down to look the site over, he had had small hope that anything would come of it. But his first rough survey had banished every doubt. Not only was the ground strewn with pieces of pottery, inscribed bricks and sculpture, but there, at the foot of the principal mound, lay a fragment of a huge statue bearing an inscription on the shoulder.

Immediately a plan of action began working itself out in de Sarzec's mind. That statue had not come from the ground on which it lay; it has rolled down from the neighboring height. If, then, he were to dig on the height, he would certainly find other relics of the civilization to which the statue belonged.

His reasoning proved entirely correct. He had barely started digging when he began to uncover an extensive building and to bring up all sorts of relics, chief among them a great carved stela of a king called Eannatum, many diorite statues of one Gudea, who had ruled an ancient city called Lagash, and two terra-cotta cylinders of the same king, each inscribed with about two thousand lines of cuneiform which, just as the scholars had prophesied, turned out to be altogether un-Semitic.

From the point of view of beauty what de Sarzec had dug up certainly did not look like much. Even the excavator did not claim that for them. The statues were rude and clumsy and some of them had no heads. Nevertheless, when de Sarzec arrived with them in Paris, the distinguished curator of Oriental Antiquities at the Louvre at once recognized their value. The statues were rude, but what did that matter? They were the art of the childhood of man, the art of a world that was old and already almost forgotten when the Assyrians took the stage. They were the work of a people hitherto unknown, a people that had ruled in Babylonia for 1500 years before the Babylonians became a power. The curator felt, however, that the proper moment had not come to ask the government for a grant. "Do not announce your discoveries yet," he advised. "Return quietly to the ruins and continue excavating . . . . "

So de Sarzec went back to dig and at the right dramatic moment the news was given out in terms that shook the archaeological world: "Since the discovery of Nineveh . . . no discovery has been made which compares in importance with the recent excavations in Chaldea."

When the statues and objects were finally unpacked
and for the first time set out in the galleries of the
Louvre, there was another to-do about them such as
there had been forty years before when Botta's sculptures had arrived from Khorsabad. De Sarzec was bom-
barded with questions about his Sumerians. Everybody
wanted to know all about this newly discovered nation
whose existence had been guessed in so curious a fashion. What race had they belonged to? Where had they
come from? What was the relation between them and
the Babylonians?

Neither de Sarzec nor anyone else could answer all
the questions; very little had yet been learned about the
mysterious ancients. But already some of the outlines of
their history were shaping, and more were to appear as
other archaeologists followed de Sarzec into Babylonia.

The history of Mesopotamia was going back and back
and back. Nineveh and Babylon were young in comparison with the cities that were now being unearthed. And
now no longer could there be any question as to how
much the Assyrians and Babylonians owed to this older,
non-Semitic race that died out all of four thousand
years ago, whose very name had been forgotten and of
whose existence the world knew nothing until three
generations ago when de Sarzec began to dig. Their architecture, especially the use of the arch, the Babylonians had adopted from the Sumerians, who first gave the
great invention to the world. The Babylonian laws—on
which were based the Hebrew laws that have so greatly

influenced our own—were built on Sumerian laws. The arts had been picked up by the Babylonians at the point where the Sumerians had dropped them. The cuneiform writing of the Babylonians was an adaptation of the Sumerian. Even the Babylonian gods were Sumerian gods except that they had different names.

Naturally, the ancient Sumerian cities from which archaeologists were digging out all this startling information were in a far more broken-down condition than the Assyrian, so that it was hard to visualize them as they once had been. But one outstanding feature all of them had certainly possessed—a ziggurat, or staged tower. This tower, it became clear after the Joint Expedition of the British Museum and the University of Pennsylvania had cleared the ziggurat of Ur (the best preserved of all), had been a very curious affair. It had looked like a series of blocks set up one on top of another, each block smaller than the one below, with steps leading to the summit, where a shrine had stood.

"What in the world," people wondered, "had this mountainous pile of brick meant to the Sumerians that they couldn't build a city without one?"

"Obviously," said one archaeologist, "a mountain."

The shrewd guess shed light on a great number of things, including the origin of the Sumerians, about which historians were all in a fog. Clearly no people who built mountains had sprung up in a plain. The Sumerians must have emigrated from a mountainous country, India perhaps. Yes, and in that country they had wor-

Restoration of the Ziggurat at Ur
(Courtesy of the University Museum, Philadelphia)

shiped their gods on the mountain tops; for in their
sculptures did they not represent their gods as standing
on the tops of mountains? Arrived in the plain, they had
found it impossible to worship their gods as they had
done at home. And so they had made tons and tons of
bricks and piled them up and built artificial mountains
on the plain, with steps all the way up to represent the
path they once had climbed.

This is what the ziggurat had been—a mountain of
God. And this had been the meaning of that most famous building in the world—the Tower of Babel.

CHAPTER XXV

Mistress of Kingdoms

THOUSANDS of years of history, literature and art had sprung from the mounds. City after city had appeared. But no one had yet rescued Babylon. "Babylonia without Babylon? Impossible!" people said. "Archaeology must give back to us 'the glory of kingdoms, the beauty of the Chaldeans' pride,' the jewel which through the years has been the symbol of pride and wealth and wickedness. We must have again the city in which the Tower of Babel stood; where the wondrous gardens hung; where the lawgiver, Hammurabi, lived; where the Children of Israel were carried to captivity; where Daniel is said to have been thrown to the lions; where Alexander died."

Without Babylon the ancient world was incomplete. Many an archaeologist had said it, and many had gone to look over the mound to which the name Babil—remnant of Babilani, the Gate of the Gods—still clung. But the task of laying open this hill was so stupendous that up to the end of the nineteenth century scarcely anyone had had the courage to do more than scratch the surface. Even the ambitious Layard had looked askance at the mound. "Nothing can be hoped for from Babil," he is reported to have said, "except with a parliamentary vote of £25,000. And if this sum should be voted, I would ask the favor of not being charged with its application."

No individual depending for the most part on his own resources could hope to conquer Babil. The challenge was too great; there was at least a quarter of a century of labor there. And yet when late in the 1890's Robert Koldewey found on Babil some fragments of enameled brick reliefs, he was consumed with a desire to resurrect Babylon. He took the fragments to Berlin. The Director-General of the Royal Museums at once recognized their importance in the history of art and encouraged the archaeologist. An expedition was assembled. In 1899 the digging began.

The Germans knew they had undertaken a stupendous task, but even they did not suppose that after fourteen years of digging with 250 men they would still be only half done. The trouble lay in the fact that the mound was piled much higher above the ruins than on other sites. Whereas in many other places excavators needed to dig only through six or ten to twenty feet to reach the ruins, at Babil they had to deal with forty to eighty feet. Having begun, however, they would not stop; they were determined that Babil should yield its secrets.

But what secrets had Babil to reveal? If Babylon did indeed lie there as they supposed, whose Babylon was it?

Not Hammurabi's. They had no hope of digging up Hammurabi's Babylon, for Sennacherib had left a blasting record of his career there. The King of the Four Quarters of the Earth had conquered the city and had set up his eldest son as king. But the Babylonians had called the Elamites to their aid, revolted against their ruler and shipped him off to Elam, there to meet the usual fate of high-born prisoners. Sennacherib had been furious. Like the onset of a raging storm he had pressed upon the enemy. And after he had butchered to his heart's content, he had wiped out every trace of Hammurabi's Babylon.

The city and its houses, foundations and walls, I destroyed, I burned with fire. The wall and the outerwall, temples, and gods, temple-towers of bricks and earth, as many as there were, I razed and dumped them into the Arahtu canal. Through the midst of that city I dug canals, I flooded its site with water, and the very foundations thereof I destroyed. I made its destruction more complete than by a flood. That in days to come, the site of that city, and its temples and gods, might not be remembered, I completely blotted it out with floods of water and made it like a meadow. . . . After I had de-

stroyed Babylon, had smashed the gods thereof, and had struck down its people with the sword . . . that the ground of that city might be carried off, I removed its ground and had it carried to the Euphrates and on to the sea. Its dirt reached unto Dilmun, the Dilmunites saw it, and terror of the fear of Assur fell upon them and they brought their treasures. . . . To quiet the heart of Assur, my lord, that peoples should bow in submission before his exalted might, I removed the dust of Babylon for presents to (be sent to the most) distant peoples, and in that Temple of the New Year's Feast, I stored (some) of it in a covered bin.

The Babylon that Robert Koldewey hoped to find was the Babylon which had risen on top of this ruin. The bloody Sennacherib had himself in the end met with blood. His own sons had murdered him, and one of them, Esarhaddon, had taken power. It was he who caused Babylon to be built again, establishing its former occupants under their own ruler, but under his, Esarhaddon's, protection. In later years Nebopolassar and Nebuchadnezzar greatly improved the city till it was said to have become the most fabulous city of the Near East. The question in the minds of the German excavators was how much of this later glory yet remained.

One of the things they were especially curious about was the fortifications. They knew they would find walls, of course—in those days a city without walls was as defenseless as an oyster without its shell—but they wondered a great deal about how extensive those walls had been. The reason they were so curious was that the famous Greek traveler Herodotus had left an astonishing account of them. He had said that in the first place there was a moat, deep, wide and full of water, that ran entirely around the city. Next, there was a wall fifty royal cubits in breadth, and in height two hundred, with a hundred gates all of brass in its circumference. But this outer wall was only the second fortification. Inside there was another wall, not much weaker than the other, though narrower.

To the excavators this sounded like preposterous exaggeration. What, then, was their amazement to find that Herodotus, at every point where archaeology could test his figures, had told only the truth! His statement about the height of the walls—three hundred feet—naturally could not be checked, because they had tumbled and crumbled badly, but in width the fortifications had been such as no other city of the ancient East could boast. Eighty-five feet of defenses had stood between the citizens and the enemies who in those days were always battering down somebody's walls. And no wonder. After the terrible fate the city had suffered at Sennacherib's hands, could any amount of wall have made the Babylonians feel secure? They had buried themselves from every possible enemy—save those within. In the end when Babylon fell it was not because its walls were battered down. It was because its people quarreled among themselves. Babylon betrayed Babylon, and the priestly party, weary of internal strife, had opened the gates to Cyrus the Mede.

But what of the glories that had sprung up behind the safety of those walls? Had the Mistress of Kingdoms been as fabulous as Herodotus had said?

Nebuchadnezzar had not restrained himself. His Babylon had indeed been a city of glitter and dazzle, of ostentation and grandeur. Like all Babylonian and Assyrian monarchs, Nebuchadnezzar had wanted to impress everyone with his wealth and power and magnificence. And so instead of charming as the Egyptian Pharaohs had done by simplicity and loveliness, he had dazzled. Lavish display had been his keynote, and in the palace it had had full sway. The brilliant approach through the Ishtar Gate was only a preparation for the effects beyond—the magnificent portal, the extensive courtyards, the throne room measuring 170 by 56 feet—while for the roof was reserved the most distinctive effect of all, the "hanging gardens" so extraordinary that their fame had gone down in history as one of the Seven Wonders of the World. In Babylon not even Marduk's temple had rivaled the palace, and when the hanging gardens had adorned it and the colorful life of the empire had passed in and out, it must have been, thought the excavators, one of the most spectacular buildings in the world.

And yet it was the ziggurat that impressed them more. The original tower of the Bible story had gone forever with Hammurabi's Babylon, but, standing probably on the site of the old tower and looking doubtless

Procession Street in the Babylon of Nebuchadnezzar. The restoration shows the Ishtar Gate in the foreground. On the roof of the palace may be seen the Hanging Gardens and in the background the temple tower.

(Courtesy of the Oriental Institute of the University of Chicago) much like it, was the ruin of another. Reverently they dug it out. A huge cube of brickwork was all that was left to remind them of what had once seemed "the essence of human presumption," but the archaeologists had no difficulty in seeing it with the eyes of the Jews of the Old Testament. They saw it towering in seven stages to a height of three hundred feet. They saw it dominant in the midst of proud palaces of priests, spacious treasuries, temples, hostelries for strangers. They saw it as its builder had intended it to appear to the world when he said, "To raise up the top of E-temenanki that it may rival Heaven I set to my hand"—less the work of men than of gods, a symbol of that greatness and power that had struck awe into the hearts of distant nations.

The great surprise of Babylon, however, and the thing which most nearly gave the Germans the key to the city's spirit, was not a building but a street. It was a street like no street the world had ever seen, a main artery through Babylon and at the same time a last defense for its people. Clearly it had been designed as a fortress. If an enemy penetrated beyond the eighty-five foot fortifications, in Procession Street he would be brought to a halt, for the massive inclosing walls, decorated with long lines of lions done on enameled brick, would prove a glittering trap. Between them the invaders would be hemmed in, while from the heights missiles would come raining down upon their heads. A terrifying street even in hours of peace, what with the lions looking as if they were marching straight upon whoever approached; a beautiful, an impressive street, mounting to a grand climax at the Ishtar Gate, vivid with enameled bulls and dragons.

But to the excavators the real wonder was the pavement itself. Its foundation was made of brick, covered with asphalt, above which a flagged causeway formed the surface of the street. The center of the roadway was paved with great flags of white limestone, the sidewalks on either hand with slabs of red breccia, the joints all being filled in with asphalt. And every stone bore upon its buried edges the following words:

Nebuchadnezzar, King of Babylon, son of Nebopolassar, King of Babylon, am I. The Babel Street I paved with blocks of shadu stone for the procession of the great Lord Marduk. Marduk, Lord, grant eternal life.

How this message of more than twenty centuries ago stirred the excavators! Babylon lay in ruins, and yet the very stones cried aloud the life that had been. How the explorers wished to be transported if only for an hour to Nebuchadnezzar's Babylon when the procession of the great Lord Marduk passed along the Sacred Way! What color there must have been, what sound, what fascinating ceremony—white-robed priests bearing the sacred image of their god, strange instruments playing, flower-decked beasts led along for the sacrifice, the excited populace following! What a poor substitute for that vivid life were these dead, dusty stones which the explorers turned reverently in their hands!

Isaiah's vision of destruction had been all too well fulfilled. Wolves had howled in the castles and the pleasant palaces, wild goats had danced there. Now pick and shovel were powerless to give back to the world "the beauty of the Chaldeans' pride." And yet how much of its glamor the message on those stones could still evoke!

PART IV

CHAPTER XXVI

Stephens Starts Something

IN these days when archaeologists are digging up everything in sight, every schoolchild knows about the Maya just as he knows about the Blackfeet, the Apaches, the Navajos, and Pawnees. A hundred years ago few Americans had heard the name. Scarcely anyone in the world was aware that once a race of Indians who had stood infinitely above the primitive savages of the North had inhabited Central America. Not that the race had been wiped out. The descendants of these cultured Indians still lived in Guatemala and Yucatan. They still spoke their ancestral tongue. But now they gave no hint of a glorious creative past. The cruelties of the Spanish conquerors and the long after-years of slavery and degradation had wiped out every trace of their original genius. No one looking into their faces or observing the ordinary round of their life could suspect that in their veins ran the blood of a people who had been the Greeks

231

of the New World. They themselves had forgotten it.

And yet the evidence lay buried all around in Guatemala, in Honduras, in Yucatan. Now and again natives whose business took them to the jungle brought back tales of the monuments they had stumbled on. They had no knowledge that these ruins were the remains of cities the Maya had built, or that already at the time when the Spaniards came the cities had been swallowed by the jungle. All they knew was that the monuments were there. They did not puzzle very much about them. Nor, for that matter, did anyone else in Central America.

In New York in the year 1839, however, there was a person with more than the usual bump of curiosity. Already this curiosity had sent John L. Stephens roaming over a large part of the world's surface. Now it was about to make him a name. He was one of the few Americans who had read an account of the abandoned cities of the Maya, and, vague and unsatisfactory as this account was, he had been greatly intrigued by it. Why, he wondered, had nobody thoroughly investigated the ruins? Why hadn't anybody sketched them or described what they looked like? Why hadn't—?

The more Stephens thought about the works of art said to be buried in the tropical jungle, the more his curiosity grew, until he determined there was nothing for it but to go to Central America and see for himself. His friend Frederick Catherwood, who had spent ten years studying the antiquities of the Old World, caught the fever too. They made plans together, got their things ready. And then, shortly before they were to leave, they heard that the Minister for Central America, who also had been on the point of setting out for that region, had died very suddenly. Stephens seized the opportunity. He applied to the Government to make use of him, with the happy result that he immediately received an appointment from President Van Buren as Special Confidential Agent from the United States to Central America.

The friends set out not without misgivings. The real object of their journey, they felt, was exploration, and they didn't want the diplomatic mission to interfere with that. But as it turned out, they need have had no qualms. Arriving in Central America the young diplomat and his artist friend found the country in the midst of a bloody civil war. What, under the circumstances, might a Special Confidential Agent hope to accomplish? What government was he to deal with, and where was he to find it if he wanted to deal with it? No question, he decided, the most diplomatic thing under the circumstances would be to go and look at the ruins. Acting on the inspiration, Stephens hired muleteers and Indian carriers and, himself and Catherwood on muleback, set out for the village of Copan, which lay in Honduras, a few miles from the Guatemalan border.

And now Stephens began to realize why travelers had not bothered about the ruins. The route into the interior—and this was the great high road to the city of Guatemala—lay through forests so impenetrable and

over mountain passes so steep and narrow and dangerous that at times every step required great physical exer-
tion. Time and again the mules sank to their bellies in
the mud, and repeatedly they fell. To walk was impossible. The slippery rocks and roots, the mud, and the
steep ascents and descents drove Stephens and his com-
panion back to their suffering mules. Bruised and covered with mud from head to foot the travelers plodded
on as in a nightmare, one misadventure following on the
heels of another. Catherwood, thrown from his mule,
muttered miserably that he would have stayed at home
if he had known it would be like this. As for Stephens,
long before the caravan had reached Copan he had concluded that all they would get out of this venture was an
epitaph reading "tossed over the head of a mule, brained
by the trunk of a mahogany-tree, and buried in the mud
of the Mico Mountain."

But it was over at last. After weary days they arrived
in the village of Copan and were at the gateway to the
ruins. On the following morning, having secured the
services of the only native who knew anything about the
ruins, they set out for the jungle in high excitement.

Not that either Stephens or Catherwood really expected to see much. Although their curiosity had been
deeply stirred by the report they had read, they were
somewhat skeptical as to what they should find, for in
their experience people always exaggerated things. They
went hoping rather than expecting to find wonders.
What was their surprise, then, when their guide, cutting

a way for them with his machete, led them to a monument far surpassing anything they had even dreamed about! They stood in utter amazement before the sculptured stone. This figure of a man curiously and richly dressed, this intricately patterned stone covered on the sides with hieroglyphics, was not the work of savages.

This was art, great art, a fierce sort of art that they couldn't quite understand but which they recognized as art of the highest kind. Stephens and Catherwood had never seen anything like it. Bewildered, stumbling, at the risk of their necks they made their way to the next monument and the next, which their guide disclosed to them by the vigorous use of the machete. For the jungle had not respected art. It had gone about its business of growing in its own ruthless way, shoving the dead aside to make room for the living. Enormous roots had pulled down beautifully sculptured stones, interlacing branches had locked others in a tight embrace and almost lifted them out of the earth, huge vines and creepers had hurled monuments flat upon the ground and bound them down.

When they had viewed fourteen such monuments, Stephens and Catherwood, glowing with excitement, turned to examine a great pyramidal structure which towered above the trees. They climbed up the steps, clambered over the ruined top, crossed a terrace, went down a flight of steps, up another, reached a broad terrace a hundred feet high and sank down on the edge of the supporting wall. They felt they had to be quiet and

Dated stones and turtle altar at Copan
(Courtesy of Carnegie Institution of Washington)

think. A mystery which they strove in vain to penetrate surrounded them. Historians had told them that only savages had peopled America. But this day's experience said otherwise. Savages had never reared these structures nor carved these stones. But who, then, were the people who had built this city? *"Quien sabe?* (Who knows?)" their Indian guide answered dully when they asked him. Neither men nor books could tell them.

The desolate city lay before them "like a shattered bark in the midst of the ocean, her masts gone, her name effaced, her crew perished, and none to tell whence she came, to whom she belonged, how long on her voyage, or what caused her destruction; her lost people to be traced only by some fancied resemblance in the construction of the vessel, and, perhaps, never to be known at all." The place where they sat—was it a citadel from which an unknown people had sounded the trumpet of war? Or was it a temple for the worship of the god of peace? The monkeys trooping in the tree tops knew as much about it as they. "All was mystery, dark, impenetrable mystery, and every circumstance increased it."

The friends exchanged a sober, meaningful glance. That glance said, "Here is a job vastly more important than diplomatic missions!" It was appalling to think that they were almost the only people on earth who knew anything about this lost world. They must make it their business to let people know. At whatever cost to health they must stay in this fever-laden jungle and "snatch from oblivion these perishing but still gigantic memorials of a mysterious people.

But how were they to go about making the drawings? The immensity of the work startled them. They couldn't possibly explore all. Their guide knew only this district, but there were certainly other monuments completely buried in the woods and entirely unknown. The woods were so dense that the only way to make a thorough exploration would be to cut down the entire forest and burn the trees, which was out of the question, of course. They must be content with doing a little. They must start by making drawings of the sculptured columns.

But even this much was very difficult. The designs were so complicated and so different from anything Catherwood had ever seen before that they were quite unintelligible to him. No wonder nobody had ever sketched the ruins! Strong light was needed to bring out the figures, and in the dense growth they could get sunlight only by cutting down all the trees around each column. How were they going to do this? They had no axe, and all the Indians possessed was the machete, or chopping knife. This instrument was all very well for shrubs and branches, but it would make slow impression on large trees.

Fortunately the explorers had been "buffeted into patience." The next morning they set Indians to the discouraging work of cutting down trees with a machete, and in the course of much time a space was cleared. The drawing frame was set up, the work of copying began. Stephens meantime undertook the task of exploring and

The Temple of Kukulcan as Catherwood sketched it
(Courtesy of Carnegie Institution of Washington)

clearing other monuments, a work that for him was filled with enchantment. "It is impossible to describe," he afterward wrote, "the interest with which I explored these ruins. The ground was entirely new; there were no guidebooks or guides; the whole was a virgin soil. We could not see ten yards before us, and never knew what we should stumble upon next. At one time we stopped to cut away branches and vines which concealed the face of a monument, and then to dig around and bring to light a fragment, a sculptured corner of which protruded from the earth. I leaned over with breathless anxiety while the Indians worked, and an eye, an ear, a foot, or a hand was disentombed; and when the machete rang against the chiselled stone, I pushed the Indians away, and cleared out the loose earth with my hands. The beauty of the sculpture, the solemn stillness of the woods, disturbed only by the scrambling of monkeys and the chattering of parrots, the desolation of the city, and the mystery that hung over it, all created an interest higher, if possible, than I had ever felt among the ruins of the Old World."

It was a project that called for heroism, but it yielded a hundredfold in joy. No hardships, neither illness, nor bad food, nor heat, nor wet, nor mud, nor insects—Catherwood had to draw with gloves on because of the mosquitoes—nor physical discomfort of any sort could tear the two from the absorbing task they had set themselves. When they had done with Copan, they traveled on to other forgotten cities. They made notes, plans, sketches. And when two years later Stephens' *Incidents of Travel in Central America, Chiapas, and Yucatan* came from the press, it contained not only an account of everything they had seen but a collection of engravings that set the country gasping.

The reading public was stunned. It came as a tremendous surprise to the great majority of people that there had ever been in America any except "ordinary" Indians. They were amazed that there had once flourished on American soil a race that could hold up its head with any of the great people of ancient times, an artistic race that built beautiful temples and palaces and carved intricate stone monuments and painted pictures, an intel-

lectual race that had gone so far as to invent a hieroglyphic writing.

Stephens' book became the most popular one of its
time. Within three months of publication it went
through ten editions. In England, in Germany, in Mexico there was such a demand for it that it had to be re-
published in those countries. Central American ruins
were on everybody's lips. A thousand questions were
asked. Who were these strange Indian artists? Where
had they come from? How did they get to be what they
were? Could it really be that they were of the same race
as the war-whooping savages who had scalped and
tomahawked the Puritans?

As time went on, a war of words began to be waged
about the Maya, to whom the great civilization was now
attributed. People said it just wasn't possible that any
Indians had developed so far all by themselves. They
must have had help from somewhere in the Old World.
Some said Egypt, because didn't the Maya build pyramids? Others said India, because weren't some of the
sculptured figures something like elephants? Every possible and impossible theory was dragged out. Back and
forth they argued, piling one piece of nonsense on top
of another. They had Carthaginians coming to America.
They had Pacific Islanders crossing the ocean in strong
canoes. And when they couldn't think of anything else,
they said the Maya were the lost Children of Israel.

To all this the majority of serious scholars had just
one thing to say: "The West has every reason to believe

it gave rise to a race as original as any in the East. While it is possible that stray boatloads of Polynesians reached the New World, a few people could not have greatly affected the culture of the Indians."

"But if what you say is true," people argued back, "how do you account for the difference between the Maya and all the other Indians? You say they all started even. You think they all came to America from the same place—Siberia—and that they all crossed to Alaska by the same bridge—the Aleutian islands. You think that perhaps ten or fifteen or twenty thousand years ago when they made that crossing they all of them knew only the same rude arts—how to make fire, how to chip stone. How then did the Maya get so far ahead of the rest? What gave them their start?"

It was easier to ask questions than to answer them. But as the years went on, the scholars could point to some basic facts. "In the first place," they said, "all the Indians didn't come to the New World at one time. They came in small bands, in waves, over very long periods of time. The earliest comers probably knew no more than how to make fire and chip stone. The later immigrants doubtless brought new arts with them—they knew how to make tools of polished stone, how to weave baskets, how to hunt with bow and arrow, they had domesticated the dog. As for the Maya, we don't know anything about their very early history, but one thing is certain: the thing that put them ahead of many other tribes was the fact that they were primarily farmers.

"It stands to reason," the scholars explained, "that the hunting Indians didn't have the same chance to create a high culture. There is no incentive to build a fine house and make lovely things to put in it if you are off to some other place next season. It is only when people settle down in cities and stay generation after generation that the arts spring up. And this, of course, is possible only when people are sure of a sufficient food supply. The Maya had that. Long centuries before, their predecessors had developed the wild corn of Mexico, *teosinte* or sacred maize, into such a dependable product that a great civilization could be built on it."

"But the Indians in New England grew corn," came the objection.

"Yes, but the Indians of New England were hunters and fishermen for the most part," the scholars replied. "Corn couldn't be depended on in the New England climate. Remember that it had to be coddled along by putting a herring or a porgee in each hill."

Strangely enough, the Maya themselves, humbly living out their lives in Yucatan and Guatemala, were slow to accept the tribute of originality with which scholars wanted to crown them; for white men had been written into their legendary tales. One of their strongest traditions was that long ago there came to their shores from afar ships bearing a race of fair-skinned beings. The sides of the ships shone like the scales on a serpent's skin, and to the natives who ran down to meet them they looked like great serpents coming swiftly toward them.

The people in the ships were tall and fair and blue-eyed and wore strange garments. And around their foreheads they had an emblem like serpents twined together. Now one of the gods whom the Maya worshiped was the Sacred Serpent. So when the natives beheld these strange serpent-crowned men in their strange serpent-like craft, they were certain that these weren't human beings at all but sons of their own Sacred Serpent. They welcomed the strangers joyfully as gods, and the Chanes, as they called the strange beings, settled down and lived with the Maya and became their teachers and their guides.

It was good argument for the opposition, this legend, and it is still argument today. For the war of words which Stephens started is not yet over. Though most people have come to believe that Maya genius accounts for everything, there are still some who doubt it, and these are very apt to follow up their argument with another: "Do you know that the Maya even called a certain place Tamoanchan—the Place Where the Serpent People Landed?"

CHAPTER XXVII

Jungle Secrets

STEPHENS and Catherwood had blazed the trail. But Central America was not Greece and no hopeful archaeologists rushed down to follow in their footsteps as they had done in Schliemann's. The reason was that excavating the Maya monuments was too hard. Archaeology in the jungle called for heroism of an exceptional sort. Very few people had it, and the result was that year by year the scholars who wanted to study Maya hieroglyphs got gloomier over the situation. How could they work out the puzzle if they had no exact copy of the puzzle to work on? When at last, forty-two years after Stephens, Alfred Maudslay went down into the jungle seven times and came out not only with a photograph and a drawing of every ruin then known, but with accurate molds of many inscriptions and even of entire monuments, the Maya enthusiasts were ready to lay wreaths at his feet. For by that time the public interest had been raised very high by a momentous discovery. The key to the hieroglyphs had been found.

All the time that the wordy war about the Maya had been going on, no one had had the least suspicion that the Maya Rosetta Stone was quietly resting in the archives of the Royal Academy of History in Madrid. In 1863 Brasseur de Bourbourg dug it out. It was a musty old book dating from the days of the Spanish conquerors and looking very much as if it hadn't been looked into for three hundred years. Now overnight certain scrawls with which it was illustrated were to turn it into a priceless treasure to be fought over and placed under glass.

The *Account of Things in Yucatan* had been written by one Diego de Landa, second Bishop of Yucatan, a Spaniard who seems to have had the most contradictory qualities in his make-up. He did his very best on a certain day in July, 1562 to destroy the culture of the Maya by ordering their books (works of the Devil!) to be burned in the public square of Mani. And yet this same destroyer possessed the soul of an archaeologist delighting in ancient lore. He made an intimate friend of the deposed King Cocom, "a man of great reputation, wise, sagacious, and learned," and took pains to get out of him all the Maya lore he knew. He even let Cocom keep one of those unholy works of the Devil in order that they might study it together. From the son of a Maya highpriest, de Landa also pumped a good deal of information. And all this he put into his *Account of Things in Yucatan* along with sketches of the hieroglyphs for the

twenty days of the Maya month and for the eighteen
months of the Maya year.

What a find these few scrawls were! Not all the gold
the Spaniards squeezed out of Mexico was worth so
much. How the scholars blessed the bishop as they
pored over the key that would unlock the secrets of the
Maya! And how, on the other hand, they reviled him
for having destroyed the books! Fortunately he hadn't
succeeded in destroying all. Three Maya books, carried
to Europe probably by Spanish soldiers, still existed.
The scholars now jumped to compare these manuscripts
with Landa's hieroglyphs. They compared both with
the stone inscriptions. And again scholarship triumphed.
The monuments began to speak. They would not tell
all their story—for even today only thirty per cent of the
signs have been worked out—but what they said was
very important: they told the date on which a monument had been set up.

To people who didn't know the facts this seemed very
little. "What," they exclaimed, "is the good of knowing
a date if you don't know what happened then? October
12, 1492. July 4, 1776. Such dates are meaningless unless
you know what historical event occurred at that time."

But being able to read the dates on the Maya monuments meant something very significant all the same.
When hardy archaeologists finally braved the rigors of
the jungle life and started to resurrect the Maya in earnest, one of the first things they learned was that the
Maya had not set up their monuments to commemorate

particular events. For a period of at least 1500 years they had set their monuments up regularly every twenty years—and in the larger cities every ten or five years. And this fact was very revealing. It made it possible to gauge almost exactly when they founded any one of their cities, when they left it to live in another, and when they abandoned their jungle empire altogether.

A history which the Maya had only indirectly written down now began to be painfully pieced together from the dates. And an astonishing story of building and abandoning it proved to be.

About the year which according to our chronology is 68 A. D. (the earliest date the archaeologists found on any monument) the Maya founded Uaxactun, the first of those jungle cities which 1500 years later so astonished the Spaniards. They lived in Uaxactun for about 120 years. Then they sent out a colony to a site about fifteen miles away, where they founded Tikal. About 424 A. D. (the last date in Tikal) they abandoned that city—or, at least, it became so unimportant that it wasn't worth while to put up any more monuments. After Tikal the Maya founded and abandoned one great city after another. And then between 530 and 629 A. D. they abandoned their empire altogether; the entire population of all the cities migrated north to Yucatan. They abandoned an empire which represented the work of a people for five or six hundred years, abandoned their temples and palaces, abandoned the farms which had made possible the building of a great civilization, and

The Maya had two systems of writing numbers. One was a series of twenty heads denoting numbers from 0 to 19. The other was a system of bars and dots. A bar stood for five, a dot for one.

(Courtesy of the Field Museum of Natural History, Chicago)

went to live in a country where the soil was poor and where there were no rivers at all.

"Why did they do it?" the archaeologists asked themselves as one date stone after another corroborated this astonishing story. "Was there a dread disease that drove them out? Was there an earthquake? Did war or fear of war cause them to migrate? Did the climate change and make the land uninhabitable? Were their crops beset with pests? Or did some religious or superstitious reason urge them to leave everything and go away?"

Some clung to one theory and some to another. But slowly most of them came to believe that the secret of all those movings and of that final great migration lay in bad farming. The Maya doubtless exhausted their soil. If their farming method was the same 2000 years ago as it is today, then the Maya used to cut down the trees and burn all the shrubbery and growth on a field before planting. The next year they didn't plant the same field, but cleared other ground and planted there, letting the first field lie fallow anywhere from two to seven years. When sufficient trees and bushes had grown back to provide fertilizer, they burned the field again and planted it. Each time they did this, however, more of the humus soil was destroyed by the fire and it required more and more years in between plantings. Finally the soil would be exhausted altogether and nothing but coarse grass would grow. To find land for their crops people had to go farther and farther away from the city until it became a burden to travel back and forth. As always happens when times are hard, the hungriest and most adventuresome went to look for a better home. They discovered Yucatan. Little by little the news filtered back; others trekked after them. Until at last nobody was left in the old home towns, and the jungle closed over them.

Duck-billed god found near Tuxtla in the State of Vera Cruz, bearing the date May 16, 98 B. C.

(Courtesy of U.S. National Museum)

CHAPTER XXVIII

Magic in the Old Empire

PETRIE had set archaeologists on the right track
when he said the idea was not so much to show
the mummy as "to show the Egyptian when he was a
mummy only in expectation." The jungle heroes felt
quite the same way about it. "It is not so much these
sculptured buildings, these stelae, these pyramids and
temples that we are here to rescue," they thought, "as it is
the forgotten artists who made them. Our chief business
with these stones is to reconstruct the Maya from them."

And so as they worked away, struggling with roots
and vines and heat and insects and fever and jungle
beasts and serpents, they tried to translate every monument into life, character, custom, idea. The carving, for
instance, with which many of the buildings of the Old
Empire were covered so that they were virtually pictures
in stone did not mean to the archaeologists simply that
the Maya had been incomparable artists. It meant to

them that many Maya had been slaves. For all that sculpture chiseled out of stone with tools of stone had required a terrific amount of time. To carve those façades and lintels and beams and altars and stelae with difficult patterns into which human and animal figures were intricately woven, thousands of skilled artists had been employed. Thousands of laborers, too, had spent their lives hauling stones, cutting stones, polishing stones. Probably in the periods between sowing and harvesting when the crops did not need much attention, the entire peasant population had been conscripted to work on the pyramids and temples. Perhaps as in Egypt at the time of the building of the pyramids, a whole nation had toiled and suffered that the work of king and priest might go forward.

The plan of the cities, again, while different for each city, was in one way alike in all the Old Empire and told the same story—that the rulers had been powerful and few and the people poor and many. The thing was self-evident. The temples, the houses of the priests, and the dwellings of the rulers and nobility all stood together in a group, forming what might be called a civic center, while out beyond, each on its little platform and numbering into the tens of thousands, had stretched the palm-thatched huts of the common people.

It looked like the simplest town plan in the world. But the excavators could easily see that a great deal of strategy had gone into its making. That plan had been devised with an eye to the greatest possible effect. The

Maya sculpture showing penitent passing a cord with thorns through his tongue

(Courtesy of Carnegie Institution of Washington)

huts of the people were low. The temples and palaces were all raised up on mounds, either natural hills sliced off at the top or artificial mounds built of rubble and neatly cased in mortar, one mound or hill often serving as the base for several temples. The general effect had certainly been awesome and had doubtless succeeded in inspiring the humility and obedience it was meant to inspire in the hearts of the simple farmers. "How wonderful," the Maya must have thought, "are those beings up there on the heights in those beautiful carved stone buildings! They are not like us. They do not dress in common loincloths the way we farmer folk do. How their brilliant feather capes and jeweled armlets and headgear of quetzal feathers glisten in the sun! They cannot be ordinary men like us. They are like the gods!"

Ceremony and pomp and ritual had clearly been the halo with which the priests surrounded themselves—many of the sculptures showed that—but magic had probably helped as much to keep them in power. They knew things about the sun and the moon and the stars that made master magicians out of them. For centuries they had applied themselves to the study of astronomy, especially to the correct measurement of time, and with such good results that they could reckon time by sun, moon and planets. They had worked out a calendar that was almost perfect (far better, indeed, than any the Old World had at that time). They had worked out also a moon calendar and exactly coordinated it with the sun calendar over long periods of time. And they could even predict eclipses.

For the display of all this "magic" the priests had taken pains to provide exactly the right setting—the steep steps of their temple pyramids. It was clear to every excavator that these made a perfect background. But nobody understood the lengths to which the priests sometimes went to enhance this setting until Oliver G. Ricketson, Jr., working for the Carnegie Institution of Washington, excavated in 1928 a certain pyramid at Uaxactun.

Among the ruins of that first Maya city, and directly opposite a row of three temples standing side by side, there stood out a pyramid-like hill about fifty feet high. It wasn't a base for a temple because it sloped up to a more or less sharp peak, although it might indeed at one time have supported a wooden hut, for there was a platform of plaster on the top. Had it been a place of human sacrifice? Doubtless, but Ricketson was interested in a different aspect of his problem. As he worked around the pyramid he kept constantly thinking of the relation in which it stood to the three ruined temples opposite. Back in 1924 he had been a member of an expedition that had gone to Uaxactun for the Carnegie Institution, and he had been much impressed by what Frans Blom, one of the directors of that expedition, had thought about this pyramid mound and the three temples standing on the mound opposite. Blom had suspected that there was some astronomical significance in their arrangement, something that had to do with the amplitudes of the sun at the equinoxes and solstices. Ricketson decided he would not let that matter remain unsettled.

Right in front of his pyramid there stood a stela on a low dais. Ricketson set up a theodolite—an instrument for measuring angles—on the center line of this stela and then set up markers on the midlines of the thresholds of the inner doorways in the three temples and took angular readings. His results were startlingly conclusive. The stela and temples had indeed been erected with a special design in view—the whole formed a huge sundial!

The Maya astronomers knew very well that the sun does not always rise and set in the same place. They had built their temples in the sun's honor accordingly. When the sun rose behind the northern front corner of Temple I, it was the summer solstice, June 21; when it rose behind the southern front corner of Temple III, it was the winter solstice, December 21; and when it rose behind the exact middle of Temple II, it was either the spring or the autumn equinox—that is, the time when day and night are of the same length, March 21 or September 22.

For what purpose had the priests gone to all the trouble of having the huge sundial built? Their simple economy had no need of exact dates. The Maya were an agricultural people. All they needed to know was roughly the time to plant and to harvest. But the priests doubtless had made a magic ceremony out of their sundial for each agricultural occasion. With awe-inspiring

*Pyramid of the grotesque faces at Uaxactun before exca-
vation*   (Courtesy of Carnegie Institution of Washington)

mystery and breathtaking display they had climbed the
pyramid and, very likely to the accompaniment of human
sacrifice, had declared from the height the command
they had received from heaven to put seed into the
ground or to bring in the harvest.

It was a great satisfaction to Ricketson to have settled
the question of the astronomical use to which temple
and pyramid and stela had been put, but it was an even
greater satisfaction to learn the secret of the pyramid itself. Even when he first began to work around it, it
seemed to him to have a mystery about it. Somehow it
looked like a pointed box that might contain something.

Pyramid of the grotesque faces excavated
(Courtesy of Carnegie Institution of Washington)

So one day he carefully dug a little into one corner and what was his delight to discover that inside the pyramid there was another pyramid. The outer crust was so badly damaged that it was really not sacrificing anything to pull the whole thing down and expose what lay inside. He set to work and soon could see that the inner pyramid was almost perfectly preserved.

It started with a low terraced platform that had stairways on all four sides. On top of this was another platform with just one stairway going up the front side. And on the sides of the stairways there were eighteen huge faces made of stone overlaid with stucco—ferocious human monster faces, eight feet square, with open slit-like mouths and great teeth in them.

One of the faces on pyramid at Uaxactun
(Courtesy of Carnegie Institution of Washington)

Ricketson had no idea why this earlier pyramid had been covered up unless it was for the sake of building a grander pyramid above it. Whether the Maya had succeeded in their purpose or not he could not tell. All he knew was that this inner pyramid was very very beautiful. Its style was strange, unlike other pyramids, and seemed to bridge the gap between the art of the Old Empire and the rude art of the predecessors of the Maya.

What was the history of those early pyramid builders? Ricketson could only guess. The stone faces would not speak their secret, and as for the dated stones, Ricketson might look in vain to them for help. Probably even if he could read all the hieroglyphs, that first monument dated 68 A. D. would have very little to tell him about history, either Maya or pre-Maya. Probably most of what it recorded was some of those astronomical phenomena which the priests were always searching the heavens for. Probably the real significance of a stela was some more of that magic which had helped the priests to remain as gods in the eyes of the people.

Pomp and ceremony, ritual and magic. Not only the pyramids, but every cut stone fallen from a ruined building carried the impression that the priests had made the most of every opportunity to dazzle and mystify. Doubtless even the "unveiling" of a stela had been a half-magical occasion—the climax to a grand fête day, when, with singing and dancing and prayers for rain and many children, the priests had reviewed the chief events that had taken place in the sky and on the earth during the last five or ten or twenty years. And the fact that the people could not read the hieroglyphs on the stela had only helped the magic along. The priests understood the value of ignorance very well. They purposely guarded the secret of writing jealously in order that the hieroglyphs might play their own little magic role with the people. But they little guessed what the price of this small bit of magic was to be—oblivion. When king and priest and noble had perished at the hands of the Spaniards, Maya culture perished too. Now only haltingly, only brokenly, only with many gaps could its history be put together again.

CHAPTER XXIX

What Happened in Yucatan

IN the New Empire the history gaps were not quite so wide as in the Old for not all the story had to be pieced together from stones. Fortunately, before Maya culture burned out altogether, it sent up a few last sparks in the form of several records of events (interspersed with prophecies, rituals, native catechisms, accounts of the creation of the world, almanacs and medical treatises), written in the Maya language but in the European characters which Maya scholars had learned from the Spanish priests.

The sacred books of the Maya of Yucatan were called the Books of Chilam Balam. They were called that after one Balam, a *chilam* (mouthpiece or interpreter of the gods), who was the last and greatest of the Maya prophets. He had lived in the last part of the fifteenth and probably the first part of the sixteenth century, and had got himself such a reputation by correctly prophesying

the coming of strangers from the East who would estab-
lish a new religion that in later times he was considered
the authority for many other prophecies with which he
had had nothing to do, for they had been uttered long
before his time. In Chumayel, in Mani, in Tizimin there
were Books of Chilam Balam. In the nineteenth century
they were ferreted out, and it was seen at once that they
were a great treasure, especially for the reason that large
parts of the books had been transcribed from hieroglyphic manuscripts that had somehow escaped the
eagle eye of Diego de Landa and his fellow zealots.

The Chilam Balam of Chumayel was of the greatest
interest to the men who were trying to piece out the history of the Maya in Yucatan. It contained an outline history of the Itza, who in times past had been one of the
three reigning families of Yucatan and actual rulers of
the great city Chichen Itza. With this as the starting
point and with additional information from others of the
Chilam Balam, together with help from archaeology and
from that old book of Diego de Landa's, the scholars
were able to work out a pretty clear outline of what had
happened in Yucatan.

As might have been supposed, the emigrants from
Honduras and Guatemala found their hands so full of
pioneering in Yucatan that it was centuries before they
produced really great art and architecture. It was a time
of cutting down trees, a time of searching for water.
They saw no rivers in Yucatan, but fortunately all
through the northern half of the country they came upon

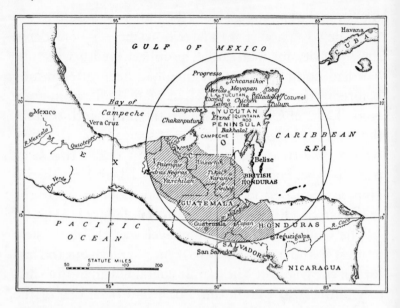

The circle encloses the region occupied by the Maya during the first fifteen centuries of the Christian era. The shaded portion, called the Old Empire region, shows where they lived for upwards of a thousand years.

(Courtesy of Carnegie Institution of Washington)

cenotes or natural wells, often of very large size. Not being geologists, the Maya did not know that under the earth and limestone of Yucatan there were numerous lakes and rivers. They were very prompt, however, to take advantage of the wells that formed wherever the earth's crust had caved in above an underground body of water, and they took advantage also of water-filled caves and water holes. And so little by little they made their farms and grew their staple crop and sank their roots deep into the soil of Yucatan.

But the genius of the Maya for art and architecture was only sleeping. Once the people had become established, it awoke anew. They began to build with fresh zeal, in a new style, majestic cities that rivaled one another in beauty, daring, magnificence. And Chichen Itza surpassed them all. Chichen Itza had an advantage over the other cities. It had two of the great natural wells so important to life in this riverless country. From them, indeed, the city took its name—Chichen Itza, Mouth of the Wells of the Itza. It became a city that grew and grew. From all over the peninsula and even from farther away people flocked to it for the sacrificial rites.

The Xiu, a people also of Maya stock, but whom the other Maya looked on as foreigners, quarreled and fought with the Itza and kept on quarreling right up until the Spaniards arrived. Sometimes the Itza had the upper hand, sometimes the Xiu. But once a league had been set up between the three great cities, Chichen Itza, Uxmal and Mayapan, and for two hundred years there had been peace. Then later again, for some trifling reason—some say because two kings loved the same woman and one of them stole the bride on her wedding night—strife broke out and the first United States of America began to go to pieces. The ruler of Chichen Itza hatched a plot against the king of Mayapan. He in turn called in Mexican allies to help him, and with their aid drove out the king of Chichen Itza and utterly routed

the inhabitants. But the war against Mayapan continued, and in 1451 the city fell and was destroyed.

After that the Maya went down, down, down. Disaster followed on disaster. A colossal hurricane swept
the country, uprooting the age-old trees. Disease struck
the crops and fruit trees. Pestilence carried off great
numbers of the people. Famine and then civil war carried off many more. And so, weakened and divided, they
were found by the Spaniards, who needed to deliver
only a final blow to crush them altogether.

In a thin web of history like this, stretching over
many centuries, it was not to be expected that any individual should have stood out greatly from among his fellows. And yet the records insisted that there had been
such a person and that he had profoundly affected the
history of the Maya.

It seems that somewhere in perhaps the twelfth or the
thirteenth century there appeared a stranger among
the Maya, a man whom the Mexicans called Quetzal-
coatl and the Maya Kukulcan. In Mexican his name
meant "Quetzal-bird-serpent," in Maya "Feathered-
serpent." He came to Chichen Itza—so legend says—as a
prisoner of war. The Maya promptly threw him into the
Sacred Well as a sacrifice to the Rain God, Nahoch-
Yumchac. But Kukulcan did not drown. At noon he was
still alive, and the Maya, according to their custom, then
fished him out. When they had offered him to the Rain
God, they had given him the rank of a god. Now in their
eyes he was divine, a living god.

So, at least, says the tradition. Whether it be true or not, this Kukulcan became the ruler of Chichen Itza and the most powerful chief in Yucatan. Everybody near and far held him as a god. Temples were dedicated to him and everywhere the feathered serpent appeared in stone. To the body of this serpent the artists gave the form of the rattlesnake. Instead of scales they gave the rattlesnake the feathers of the sacred quetzal bird.

Kukulcan made Mayapan his capital city and established peace in Yucatan. And then, at the height of his power, just as suddenly as he had appeared among the Maya, so suddenly he disappeared.

"Who was this mysterious Kukulcan?" archaeologists pondered as they worked around the temples built in his honor. Was he just a Mexican captain? But in that case, why in one portrait did the Maya represent him with a beard? The Indians had very scanty face hair, and the Maya scalded theirs off. Was Kukulcan a white man? He certainly looked like one, very much like Uncle Sam in fact. Was he a Norseman? Were there perhaps two Kukulcans, one a god and one a hero?

Intriguing guesses which nobody could either prove or disprove! Kukulcan was still half shadow. Only with the coming of the Spaniards could any scholar feel himself on sure ground, for only in the Spanish records did the Maya come out into the full light of history.

Strangely enough, according to those records it does not appear that the Spaniards had everything their own way from the start. On the contrary, "the first round" went altogether to the Maya.

In 1511 twenty Spanish sailors and two women were driven ashore near Yucatan. Several of the men and both the women soon afterward died, while the rest fell into the hands of the Maya. They did not take kindly to the Spaniards. Five of the strangers were immediately sacrificed in the usual fashion by having their hearts torn from their living bodies. Afterward, to the horror of the captives, the bodies of their sacrificed comrades were served up and eaten at a ceremonial banquet. When they themselves were thrust into wooden cages, they knew they had only a similar fate to look forward to. All but two were sacrificed in this way.

These two, a pious cleric named Geronimo Aguilar and a sailor named Gonzalo Guerrero, had been considered too lean for sacrifice. They were consequently left in their cages to fatten. But they had no intention of dying meekly. While the attention of their guards was somewhere else, the two Spaniards broke their way out of their cages and escaped into the jungle. Even the terrors of the jungle were better, they thought, than the horrible death that awaited them if they stayed.

By day Aguilar and Guerrero lay low, by night they traveled. After several terrible days and nights, they fell in with a friendly Maya band. These Maya were ready to spare them because they had escaped from a band which was their own enemy too. Both men, of course, were made captive. Aguilar was later traded to another band and subsequently got back to the invading Spaniards. But Guerrero stood by the Maya. He taught them everything he knew and became in every way a Maya himself. He pierced his ears sugar-bowl-handle fashion and inserted ear plugs into the holes as the Maya did. He could not flatten his head like the natives because that should have been done in babyhood, and he could not squint fashionably because nobody had hung a wax pellet between his eyes when he was young, and it was too late to prevent his beard from coming by applying hot cloths, but the Maya maidens apparently let that pass. Anyway, he married the chief's daughter, a beautiful, accomplished and cultured girl, and became the most honored citizen of the tribe.

When the Spaniards heard where Guerrero was, they sent word to him to come and join them. They could not suppose that a Spaniard would choose to live with the Maya if he had a chance to get back to his own people. They were astounded when Guerrero answered them by making war, and making it in the European fashion, for he had taught the Maya even that. For eight years he successfully led the Maya against the invaders. Had he not died at the end of that time, perhaps the whole history of America might have been different.

But Guerrero died, and not long after his death power passed from the Maya. Though the Maya stubbornly continued to resist the invaders, the Xiu allied themselves with the Spaniards and thus helped to bring about the subjection of all the tribes. The Spaniards crushed the natives under an iron heel. All the cruelties of the Spanish Inquisition were used to subdue them. They suffered every imaginable torture. "Then," say the old Maya chronicles, "began the execution by hanging, and the fire at the ends of our hands. Then also came ropes and cords into the world. Then the children of the younger brothers passed under the hardship of legal summons and tribute." Their rulers deposed, their priests killed, their religion forbidden, their books burned, with appalling swiftness their culture vanished. In a few years the white men accomplished what centuries of war and pestilence and famine had not been able to do.

CHAPTER XXX

Moonlight over Chichen Itza

OF all the explorers who have labored to bring the Maya out of the darkness, nobody has accomplished so much as E. H. Thompson. He spent more than forty years in Yucatan doing things hardly anyone else would have had the courage to do. His adventures left him a little the worse for wear, to be sure. A poisoned rat trap set by Indians resulted in a lameness in one leg. Diving in the Sacred Well of the Itza made him slightly deaf. Several bouts with jungle fever robbed him of his hair. But looking back at the full years, Thompson had no regrets. "I have spent my substance in riotous exploration," he said, "and I am altogether satisfied."

Thompson came to Yucatan in a curious fashion—as he put it, "by the Lost Continent of Atlantis." He had always been an archaeologist after a fashion because the New England of his boyhood was sprinkled thick with Indian relics and to his mind no thrill was equal to finding a fashioned stone, unless it was the thrill of depositing it in the local museum. But one day he got hold of Stephens' *Incidents of Travel*. It opened his eyes to Indian relics such as he had never conceived of. He was tremendously excited. He read all the accounts of Maya civilization he could find, trying to make up his mind whether these wonderful Indians were indeed brothers to that simple folk whose arrowheads and stone pestles he had donated to the museum. He didn't think they could be. But if not, where had they come from? He jumped to a theory, wrote it up in an article which he called "Atlantis Not a Myth," and sent off his contribution to *Popular Science Monthly*. The civilization of the Maya, he suggested, was a broken branch of the civilization that once upon a time existed on the continent of Atlantis, that continent which is supposed to have stretched where the Atlantic Ocean now flows and which, according to Plato, sank out of sight in a day and a night.

The theory was daring and it attracted attention. Some time afterward the president and vice-president of the American Antiquarian Society decided young Thompson was the very person who ought to fill the post of consul to Yucatan, and neatly arranged the matter for him, giving him to understand that he was to devote all possible time to exploration of the ruined cities and to the study of the Maya of the present day.

Thompson could not suppress his joy. If ever anyone was "in the white heat of enthusiasm" for the work before him, it was he. He was ready for all the rigors of the jungle that Stephens had described, and from the beginning made up his mind he would not pamper himself in any way. Although he had a wife and two months' old daughter, he would live as much as possible with the Indians, traveling "light," eating the food they ate, learning their language, winning their friendship, working on the ruins by day and listening to Indian tales around the campfire at night.

From 1885 on for nearly a quarter of a century as consul he did not change his plan. Living from first to last the life of an Indian, Thompson traveled from one end of Yucatan to the other. He visited every known ancient city and temple center. He made many valuable researches, including the discovery of several cities until then unknown to the world. He gave himself to his work so completely that people said he was impractical. And through it all, if "the white heat of enthusiasm" cooled at all, it was only because at the back of his mind Thompson was cherishing a dream for which he wanted to reserve his brightest spirit.

When he was getting together material for his article, "Atlantis Not a Myth," he had come across Diego de Landa's famous *Account of Things in Yucatan*. He was fascinated by everything in the musty old volume, but one thing in particular caught his interest above all else. It was what the bishop had to say about the Sacred Well of the Itza.

"From the court facing these theaters (two stone plat-

Maya vase from Guatemala
(Courtesy of University Museum, Philadelphia)

forms in front of the main temple)," the bishop had written, "a broad handsome causeway led to a well about twice a stone's throw distant. Into this well it was their custom to cast living men as a sacrifice to the Gods in times of drought; and it was their belief that they did not die, although they never saw them any more. They also threw in many other things of precious stone and articles which they highly prized. Thus if this land had contained gold, this well would hold the largest part of it, so devoted were the Indians to it."

Thompson could see the whole vivid ceremony. He imagined the Maya filing in solemn procession down the steep steps of the Temple of Kukulcan and along the Sacred Way, he heard the sound of their drums beating,

The vase on preceding page in extension, showing a dignitary carried in a litter and followed by porter bearing the baggage, which is done up in a jaguar skin and carried by a tump-line across the forehead. The men behind may be canoemen carrying paddles.

(Courtesy of University Museum, Philadelphia)

their whistles blowing, their flutes wailing, he saw them casting captive warriors and beautiful maidens and all sorts of precious objects into the pool to propitiate the angry god who, they believed, lived down in its depths. And he could not stop thinking about it. He simply could not get "the thought of that grim old water pit and the wonderful objects concealed within its depths" out of his mind. Then and there he had determined that some day he would explore that well and wrest its secret from the bottom.

When he became consul, as soon as he could manage

it he paid a visit to Chichen Itza. It was an unforgettable experience. A lifetime of exploration could not wipe out the impression his first sight of Kukulcan's city made on him.

It was a moonlight night. For days he had been traveling through the jungle. He was worn out, nodding over his horse's head. Suddenly he heard an exclamation from his guide. The Indian was pointing up ahead.

Thompson raised his eyes and instantly came wide awake. High up before him loomed what seemed to be a huge Greek temple on top of a very steep hill. It seemed to him massive, like a fortress. It seemed to grow bigger and bigger the nearer he approached. He felt "an actual physical pain" as if his heart "skipped a few beats and then raced to make up the loss." He recognized it as the Temple of Kukulcan.

Tired out as he was, he could not think of lying down. His guide had curled up and gone to sleep as soon as he had unsaddled his horse. Thompson left him sleeping and climbed painfully up the steep temple stairway. It was overgrown with trees and shrubs. By the time he reached the platform eighty feet above the ground, he was panting. But there before him was the sanctuary. He looked in through the forty-foot doorway, and inside could dimly make out intricate carved bas-reliefs. The beauty, the wonder, the mystery of this temple of a forgotten faith entered into him. "Is it to be wondered at," he said afterward, "if my knees shook just a little and if I glanced apprehensively over my shoulder, awaiting the terrible majestic wrath of the god whose temple was profaned by the eyes of an unbeliever?'

He turned slowly and looked on the dead city. All about him were other ruins. A dozen pyramids crowned with buildings gleamed in the moonlight. It was all ghostly whiteness and inky blackness.

Then suddenly his eyes were caught and held by a broad raised roadway that led straight from the temple to a great black pool overgrown with trees. He stood breathless and frozen to the spot. In a flash he understood. He could only look and look. This ribbon of road was the Sacred Way. That black, overgrown pool was the Sacred Well. In its "murky depths even then might lie the pitiful bones of many once lovely maidens sacrificed to appease a grim god. What untold treasures this grisly well might hide! What tragedies had been enacted on its brink!"

Thompson had been sure before. Now there was no shadow of hesitation. Here in Chichen Itza lay his life-work. When he turned his back on the city of Kukulcan, it was with the idea that one day he would go back and stay there until he had mastered its secrets.

Many years were to pass, however, before that day came. Other researches, other explorations were to hold him. But at last Thompson found himself in a position to carry out his dream. Drawing all the savings of twenty-five years out of the bank, he bought the abandoned plantation which included within its limits the ruins of Chichen Itza and its Sacred Well, and settled down to experience the greatest adventures of a life that was all adventure.

CHAPTER XXXI

The Well Gives Up Its Secret

THOMPSON had long ago decided that the well of clear water which the Maya had used for drinking purposes held no interest for him. It was the gloomy, murky pool that drew him. For days and weeks after he had purchased the ruined plantation he was a frequent "worshiper" at the little shrine on the brink of this well. He pondered, he mused, he calculated, he made measurements, he took soundings. He could not keep away from the spot although he knew very well that he could not immediately begin on his great project.

There was so much else that needed to be done! Chichen Itza at the height of its power had been a very great city. The ruins of the stone buildings covered fully three square miles. Carved and square stones in countless thousands and fallen columns by the hundreds lay scattered all over the place. Formless remains of huge buildings stood all about him, and seven great structures of carved stone and mortar still towered erect. There was so much work begging to be done that it seemed ridiculous to try first of all to solve the mystery of the Sacred Well. But Thompson never for a moment lost sight of the object with which he had bought the plantation. Often and often he stood over the Sacred Well and gazed into its murky depths, dreaming of the treasures that lay below and imagining the sacrificial rites.

The Sacred Well evoked everything that was mysterious and terrible. It was oval in shape, about 187 feet across at its greatest width, and its sides were dark and rugged and very steep. The basin was of weathered rock. Thompson measured eighty feet straight down before his line touched the surface of the water. What a spectacle that sacrificial rite must have been! Flower-decked maidens, the most beautiful in the land—brides for the grim Nahoch-Yumchac—hurled far out over the well's edge and hurtling through the air eighty feet before they struck the water!

At last a time came when Thompson could wait no longer to carry out the plan he had formed: he would dive into the well and bring up whatever evidence of sacrifice lay in its depths. It was a mad venture. He knew it. He was one lone man, he had little money, he had not much mechanical skill, the danger was great, the chance of success small. And yet he felt he must go through with it. If he did not at least make an attempt to bring up the relics, he would continue for the rest of his life to be haunted by the idea. And his faith in his project was strong. Somehow he felt that his quest would not be in vain, that he would make the well yield up its treasures!

It happened at this time that he was called to the United States for a scientific conference. The session over, Thompson took the opportunity at an informal gathering to tell in his quiet way the tradition about the Sacred Well and to explain how he meant to prove it. His friends stared at him as though he had in so many words announced that he was going to take his own life. "No person can go down into the unknown depths of that great water pit and expect to come out alive," they protested when they had caught their breath. "If you want to commit suicide, why not seek a less shocking way of doing it?"

But they could argue and throw up their hands all they wanted to. Thompson had made up his mind. He departed for Boston to get some financial help and—quite as important—a dredge and some lessons in deep sea diving. He knew very well that if the treasures actually lay in the well, they did not lie within a diver's reach. Mud and leaves and rock and muck had been accumulating on top of them for hundreds of years. A great deal of preparatory work must be done before he could hope to descend in a diving suit and come up with anything more than muck. But he prepared himself now for the last delicate task.

As soon as he got back to Chichen Itza he began operations. He had already found out where the "fertile zone" of the Sacred Well was. He had worked that out by making dummies of wood about the size and weight of the average native and hurling them into the water. The point at which they struck had become for him the more or less exact spot in the great pool where the sacrifices were most likely to be found. Now he set up the dredge in such a position as to reach this "fertile zone."

The gaping steel jaw swung out, bit into the deposit, and brought up the first cartload of wood punk, dead leaves, broken branches. Then it swung out again and repeated the process. "For days," Thompson wrote, "the dredge went up and down, up and down, interminably, bringing up muck and rocks, muck, more muck." It went on and on. Now the huge teeth would bring up a tree trunk, then again the bones of a deer, of a jaguar, then muck, muck and more muck. It seemed endless. It exhausted even Thompson's patience. His optimism began to waver before the hills of muck that were piling up. He was beginning to think that maybe he was all wrong, that maybe there was nothing down in the well after all.

"Is it possible," he asked himself, "that I have let my friends into all this expense and exposed myself to a world of ridicule only to prove what many have contended, that these traditions are simply old tales, tales without any foundation in fact?"

And then one day when the dredge came up, there lay on top of the chocolate-colored muck two yellow-white round objects. They seemed to be made of some resin-ous substance, and Thompson was bold enough to taste one. Then he put a piece into some lighted embers, and immediately a wonderful fragrance filled the air. Thompson's heart began to pound with delirious joy. There flashed across his mind like a ray of bright sunlight something he had read in the Maya chronicles: "In ancient times our fathers burned the sacred resin—pom— and by the fragrant smoke their prayers were wafted to their God whose home was in the Sun." Those yellow-white balls were Maya incense!

That night for the first time in weeks he slept soundly and long.

After that for months scarcely a day passed without something of great interest coming up in the dredge— temple vases and incense burners, arrowheads, lance points, axes, hammer stones, disks of copper, bells, disks and pendants of gold, fragments of jade and—most revealing of all—the skeletons of young women and men. In every detail Thompson was showing the old traditions to be true.

Then came a day when the dredge came up with slivers of rock bottom in its teeth. That meant that it had done as much as it could and that now human hands must search in the crannies and crevices of the bottom for the treasure that remained. So every day Thompson donned his diving suit and descended into the Sacred Well to add to his hoard. When he had finished, not only had he proved beyond dispute that the traditions were right, but he had collected a very great treasure, over three hundred separate gold objects—five golden basins and cups, forty flat dishes, twenty rings, a hundred bells, bucketfuls of broken bits of gold, and so on—a treasure worth several hundred thousand dollars. And then there were, besides, hundreds of jade beads, and pendants, and other ornaments of jade, and turquoise inlay work, and statues, and pottery, and sacrificial knives, and beautifully fashioned spearheads, and throwing sticks.

It was a wonderful hoard. It told more about the Maya people than any other discovery that had ever been made. Perhaps, as some people hold, it was the most amazing archaeological find of this century, perhaps it was even greater than Tut-ankh-Amen. And a man's dream and a man's faith had given it to the world.

CHAPTER XXXII

Adventures Inside a Pyramid

IF anyone had asked Thompson what he considered his greatest achievement in Chichen Itza, of course he would have said the Well of Sacrifice. And after that? After that the High-Priest's Sepulcher.

It happened one day when Thompson was busy excavating a small temple that stood on top of a forty-foot pyramid. He was clearing the floor of this temple when he suddenly perceived in the very center of it two large, smoothly finished stone tiles. Thompson had never met with anything like that before. Did it mean that treasure lay underneath? He carefully pried up the tiles and to his surprise found himself looking down into a large, square shaft. The walls of this shaft were very peculiar. They were made of stones, neatly cut and so laid as to overlap one another like clapboards. What on earth could that shaft have been made for? Thompson could not wait to investigate.

The first step before getting down, however, was to get the present occupant of the shaft out. Twelve feet down on the floor a fourteen-foot boa constrictor was writhing around, and it looked as if it was going to defend its squatter's rights against all comers. Archaeology for the moment could not be peacefully pursued. Thompson turned hunter and came out victorious.

Now he could safely let himself down and examine what the great serpent had been lying on. It was a heap of half-eaten human bones. It looked as if two people had been buried there, one on top of the other. And that was all there was.

Almost with a sense of disappointment Thompson cleared the mess, and then, as he was picking up the last few bones he saw in the flooring a loose stone tile. He lifted it just as before, and just as before found himself looking into a shaft grave. He moved the skeleton and quickly examined the floor beneath. There were the tiles again. Below, another grave. Thompson was getting more and more bewildered the deeper down in the pyramid he went. What on earth was the meaning of these graves one above the other? He cleared the fourth grave. Sure enough, on the floor under the bones, more tiles. Five graves one on top of another. By this time Thompson had reached a level that was even with the base of the pyramid, and as he knew that the pyramid itself stood on solid limestone rock, he expected that now he had come to the bottom of the mystery. What was his amazement, then, when he again beheld the familiar stone tiles! Barely able to control his excitement, he raised them, and there before him was a series of steps hewn out of the living rock and leading into a rock-hewn chamber.

There is nothing so mysterious as steps going right down into the ground. No one can find such a stairway without thinking of magic, of Aladdin and his wonderful lamp. Thompson felt he was taking part in a tale of enchantment. Almost anything, he felt, might happen now. But he could not wait for a genie to appear. There was work to be done. The steps and the chamber into which they led were filled with wood ashes. They had to be cleared, and the only way it could be done was by the excavator's lying flat on his back, pushing his feet ahead of him through the ashes, then heaping the ashes up in baskets and passing them up over his head to his workmen, who in turn passed them up the shaft to Thompson's young sons, who stood above on the platform. Thompson threw himself into the work, and as he dug away with hands and feet, here and there he could see the sheen of polished jade.

After some time he had cleared enough space to make it possible for four of his men to come down, too. He was pretty tired by now and was glad to see that his feet rested against the end of the cave.

"We'll consider this a day's work," he said to his men. Then he surveyed a stone slab that seemed to rest lightly against the wall right between his feet and added, "I'll look under the stone to see if any pieces of jade are there and then we'll go."

He grasped the stone slab with both hands and pulled. Almost of itself it fell back, showing a large, black hole in the floor beneath. And out of this hole came a gust of cold air that made their flesh creep. At the same instant all the candles were blown out. And there Thompson stood "in utter darkness in the bowels of the earth, balanced over a hole leading into who knew what depths and blackness."

"O Don Eduardo," one of the natives uttered in a hollow voice when he could speak at all, "this is surely the mouth of Hell." And the others took up the cry.

"Not so," Thompson answered, struggling hard to keep his balance and find the right words to say. "Since when has the mouth of Hell given forth a breath as cold as this wind?"

The reply was the very one that could convince the natives. Hell wasn't as near as they thought, and as the distance grew, their courage returned. They dragged Thompson back from the pit. Then they threw their coats and hats over the hole to keep the wind down and lit their candles again. They waited a minute. Then they slowly removed the garments and waited till the rush of air had stopped. Thompson leaned over the opening and peered in. A circular well, goodness only knew how deep, had been cut straight down. He lit a small lantern, tied it to the end of his metal tapeline, and let it down. Fifty feet!

The next day was spent preparing for the descent and

on the day after, with a knife between his teeth for all contingencies and a lantern in his hand, Thompson had himself lowered by a rope. He had scarcely touched bottom on a heap of earth near the center of the chamber when he saw that his high expectations would be realized. Right at his feet was a bead of jade over five inches in circumference, beautifully formed and so polished that it gleamed under the light of his lantern. Close beside it was a beautiful jade amulet, and a little to one side the fragments of a vase made of some translucent material resembling alabaster. It had been filled with jewels of jade, and these were now scattered about in the mound of earth together with objects of mother of pearl, with fragments of a pearl necklace, and vases and urns.

Thompson had been certain before that he had uncovered the last resting place of a priest of very high rank. But now that he saw these treasures that had been buried beneath ninety feet of earth and rocky crust, the mysterious assurance came to him that this was "not merely the tomb of a great priest, but the tomb of *the* great priest, the tomb of the great leader, the tomb of the hero god Kukulcan, he whose symbol was the feathered serpent." It was only an intuition, to be sure, and one that entirely disregarded the tradition that Kukulcan had gone back to Mexico, but Thompson clung to it nevertheless. As for the other graves, he would not venture to make an assertion. He could only wonder and guess. Were they those of the lesser priests of the same temple? Had they died a natural death? Or had they been killed when the High-Priest died so that they might continue to minister to him in the afterlife?

It was a mystery, a mystery among other mysteries that would perhaps never be solved. There was the jade, for instance. Where had it come from?

It was very clear to Thompson that the Maya had greatly prized the stone, prized it even above gold, in the same way that many ancient peoples have done. To the Indians as to others it had had inestimable value because of its color, the color of life, of green, of growing things. The Maya had used it, doubtless, for amulets, it had taken part in their Sun and Serpent worship, their kings and priests had given and received bits of it as priceless tokens. When they had thrown it into the Sacred Well, they had made to their grim god the greatest sacrifice in their power save only that of life itself. But where had they found their jade?

Thompson could not help thinking, as he examined the sacred beads of the High-Priest, of that article he had written so long ago, the article by means of which he had come to Yucatan. The theory of a lost continent of Atlantis—which now that he was older and wiser he would not dare to put forth so boldly—was a very convenient one so far as this same jade was concerned. If the Maya had indeed brought it with them from Atlantis, that would explain its presence in a region where there are no jade deposits and on a continent where the only source of supply was thousands of miles away in British

*The most beautiful piece of Maya sculpture known to us.
It has been badly weathered by a thousand years of lying
in a tropical jungle of Guatemala.*

(Courtesy of University Museum, Philadelphia)

Columbia and Alaska. And it would explain, too, why
the jade was always being cut into smaller and smaller
bits. Once, Thompson theorized, its supply had not
been limited. The Maya could afford to make quite large
objects of it. Then the supply had suddenly stopped.
When Atlantis in a day and a night had sunk out of
sight, there was nothing for it but to cut their jade objects into smaller and smaller ones.

It was all just a theory, of course, but it was fascinating to speculate about, and under the circumstances
anybody might be forgiven for letting imagination run
away with him. The solid fact itself was so mysterious
that it naturally set the mind on flights of fancy. The
grave of the High-Priest might have been a tale told by
Scheherazade: "In the middle of the jungle on top of a

Maya sculpture restored
(Courtesy of University Museum, Philadelphia)

pyramid there stands a temple. Go up into that temple and in the floor you will see two tiles. Lift them. Beneath there will be a shaft and in it five graves, one above the other. Go down into those graves and under the last grave there will be a stone staircase. It leads to a chamber cut in the rock. At the end of the chamber you will see a loose stone. Move it aside. Beneath there will be a deep well. Go down into that well, and there you will find the treasure of the High-Priest."

CHAPTER XXXIII

Greeks of the New World

WHEN Thompson first came to Chichen Itza, it was a jungle, a wilderness of tumbled ruins. Today it is a show-place to which Mexico and America point with pride, for the glory of the Maya has been at least in part restored. Dozens of men have worked to rescue the fallen temples, the pyramids, the so-called observatory, the ball court where once the Maya played a game something like our basketball. By the joint efforts of the Mexican Government and the Carnegie Institution of Washington many of those things which Thompson dreamed of doing and could not possibly have done alone have been carried out.

Today the dread temple to which he climbed on that moonlight night and from the pyramid platform of which he caught his first sight of the Well of Sacrifice is fully restored on two of its sides, the other two being left purposedly untouched. Every stone on the reconstructed sides has been put back into the very niche it occupied in the great days. The temple stands now impressive and serene, a wonderful symbol of the glory that was Maya.

Not far from it stands the so-called Temple of the Warriors. This temple was also sacred to the Feathered Serpent, but not to confuse it with the Temple of Kukulcan, Earl Morris, who did the excavating, named it the Temple of the Warriors. He called it that because on some of the pillars inside were carved warriors with their spears upright before them. It was nothing but a mound, this temple, when the Carnegie Institution began its work. Now, after a thousand labors and a thousand surprises—one of which, exactly as in the case of the Temple of Kukulcan, was the finding of a hidden temple inside the pyramid—it stands in all its indescribable beauty, a deathless tribute to the unknown warriors who in an unknown battle, in an unknown war, against an unknown enemy, in an unknown year, perhaps gave their lives that their nation might live.

"Pen cannot describe or brush portray," says Thompson, "the strange feelings produced by the beating of the tropic sun against the ash-colored walls of those venerable structures. Old and cold, furrowed by time, and haggard, imposing and impassive, they rear their rugged masses above the surrounding level and are beyond description."

All the dead cities of the Maya cannot be rescued as Chichen Itza has in part been. Too much has been de-

*Temple of the Warriors at Chichen Itza before
excavation*   (Courtesy of Carnegie Institution of Washington)

stroyed by time, and, besides, it would be too vast a task
to bring two empires into being. But Chichen Itza alone
is enough to show what glorious builders the Maya
were. They were hampered in many ways. They had to
make their walls very thick to support their roofs because they did not know the secret of the keystone arch.
They had no beasts of burden to transport their heavy
stone. They did not have the wheel or any mechanical
device. But their genius and their will found a way to
overcome every difficulty.

As for their high achievements in other fields of the
mind, any one of their dated stones tells the story. They
were supreme sculptors. They were supreme artists.

Temple of the Warriors after excavation
(Courtesy of Carnegie Institution of Washington)

They were perhaps the most original people who ever lived. They not only invented a hieroglyphic writing, but they invented two systems of numbers, one of which we might compare with our Arabic numbers and one with the Roman. They invented also a symbol for zero and a place value system of reckoning. They manipulated vast figures. They were first-class astronomers. They calculated time so perfectly that for 2148 years their calendar ran without the loss of a day.

For all their genius, they did make that one terrible mistake of withholding knowledge from the people and making culture the privilege of the few—priests, kings, nobles. If only de Landa had not burned the books! Or if only some of those which rebellious priests hid from Spanish eyes would come to light.

It is every explorer's dream to find one and once Thompson almost did. A native happened to tell him that some years before he had come upon a sealed vase in an ancient grave. He was sure there was treasure in it—gold, jewels—and he was terribly disappointed when he found that it contained nothing but a kind of paper.

At the word "paper" Thompson nearly jumped out of his skin.

"What kind of paper was it?" he demanded.

"Just a scrap of paper folded up," the native answered, "with what looked like a lot of little red and black monkeys painted on it."

Now this was a very good description of a Maya book. A great many of the Maya hieroglyphic signs were in the form of faces of one sort or another, and the books had looked very much like a paper painted on both sides and folded in accordion pleats.

Thompson got all hot and cold over it. What had the man done with the paper?

He had taken the vase home and put it behind the altar. "Where it is now God only knows," he said.

"If you show me that paper, I'll give you a fine horse and a still finer saddle," Thompson promised, and now the Indian was as excited as he was. They hurried off to the village. But it all ended in nothing. The woman of the hut had destroyed it in some housecleaning operation, and all that was left of the find was the vase.

That is the sort of thing that is always happening in archaeology. But we do not have to stop hoping and dreaming. Archaeologists are bringing about so many miracles that there is good chance of recovering much of what has been lost. Any day a lucky explorer may give us the key to the unknown Maya hieroglyphs. Any day a hero in a tropical helmet may tell us surely why the Maya trekked to Yucatan. We may yet learn who were those Chanes who came in Serpent Ships and taught the Maya. We may yet know who was the hero Kukulcan.

Looking Forward

THEY say that Alexander wept because he feared there would be no worlds left for him to conquer. A sad ambition! Better had Alexander sighed for conquests of another kind—but then, that was long ago.

Certainly today no one need weep for lack of worlds to conquer, and of all people the archaeologist least. For the whole earth is his province; wherever man has lived and left the work of his hands, be it a rudely chipped arrowhead or an exquisite jewel, there he may dig—there is his world to conquer. The fathers of archaeology, for all their thrilling discoveries, have left so much undone that a hundred years of concentrated effort will not see it finished. Indeed, every new find—and there is report of one practically every week—only shows how little we yet know of man's past, how much more there is to be discovered.

There are the British Isles, for example. Archaeologists have been pushing man back and back until now it seems he has been happily living in Britain for something like five hundred thousand years. And as for that little known person, the ancient Briton, who had been thought of as a downright savage, he, it seems, was no such thing, but a creator of a very high order who had more feeling for art than the Romans who conquered him. The British Isles are full of surprises. No one can possibly predict what may yet come from there.

And so with other lands. De Sarzec started something in Chaldea to which no one can see any end. Only so recently as 1927 the Joint Expedition of the British Museum and the University of Pennsylvania came upon a tomb that almost overshadowed everything Sumerian found before. It was that of a king and his queen, one Shub-ad, who had apparently died after her husband and been buried with him. Never had such a sight met an explorer's eyes. About 3200 B. C. there had been a funeral in which sixty-five persons had perished with their king, followed by another in which twenty-five had died with their queen. To all appearance they had died voluntarily, for there were no signs of struggle. There they lay, the women side by side in a long row, dressed in the elaborate costumes and headdresses they had put on for that last gruesome ceremony. At the end of the row was a gold-crowned harpist with a harp. Beyond, a sledge decorated with gold and precious stones, and in front of it the skeletons of two asses. Beside them lay their grooms, and farther on six royal guards with their copper spears and helmets. Beyond these again, two ox-wagons, and more attendants and soldiers. The king's tomb had been robbed, but the queen's was untouched, and it revealed exactly the manner in which over five thousand years ago she had been prepared for the world to come. As for the objects buried in the graves, they were as amazing as the final ceremony itself. The wealth of gold and silver cups and bowls showed an artistry that was superb, a skill of which the Sumerians hadn't even been suspected, while the harp was a thing to gasp at.

Oh, there is an infinite deal that we don't know. The

Headdress of Queen Shub-ad found at Ur
(Courtesy of University Museum, Philadelphia)

tombs of the Trojan kings are yet to be found. And there is the whole story of the Hittites to work out, that people who about 1500 B. C. built a great empire and were the strongest power in Asia Minor. Where did they come from? Exactly of what race were they? Thousands of their cuneiform tablets have been found at Hattosas, now the Turkish village of Baghaz-Keui, and the contents of those tablets are of tremendous interest. In them there is repeated mention of a people called the Ahhiyava, who, scholars have shown, are none other than the Achaeans of Homer. What is the whole story of those famous sea-raiders who harried and despoiled not only the Trojans but the Hittites as well?

Then there are Greece and the Greek lands. For all the persistent digging that has been going on on the peninsula for over a hundred years, Greece hasn't begun to be exhausted. Even the much explored Acropolis of Athens is still a happy hunting ground, and in other parts of the city anyone who starts to build a house is quite apt to chance on a historic find.

As for the Mycenaean civilization, Schliemann only opened wide the door. Many a rich tomb teeming with lore awaits the pick and spade. Not far from Mycenae, on the ancient citadel of Mideia, Swedish scholars nearly matched the Schliemann find when in 1926 they opened the unrifled tomb of a king, a queen and a princess. Everything in richest splendor was there—just as when it had been laid away in the fourteenth century B. C.

Tempting possibilities, too, lie in the ancient Greek colonies. Hundreds of these were established by the Greek cities, and they have but just begun to be excavated. The Balkans are fertile ground. The ancient peoples of that region were not blind to the arts of their neighbors the Greeks. In the fourth, fifth and sixth centuries B. C. many a glorious work of art was transported northward for the enjoyment of beauty-loving chieftains. Somewhere those treasures lie hidden in forgotten tombs.

Nor has Italy yielded all its secrets, much as it has been worked. Even Rome, Pompeii and Herculaneum are not finished, while the Etruscans still remain a puzzle in Italian history. That artistic people has left hundreds of inscriptions in a language unlike any in Europe, so that although the writing is in Greek characters, we cannot yet fully translate it. Where did the Etruscans come from? Did they have any connections with the Su-

Gold cups from Ur
(Courtesy of University Museum, Philadelphia)

merians? The Etruscans used to divine the future by examining the livers of slain beasts. Liver divination is a very rare way of foretelling the future, but it was the way of the Sumerians and quite common in Asia Minor. What is the story on it?

Persia has hardly been touched as yet. Although the ruins of Persepolis have been largely cleared by an American expedition and the ramps and staircases and battlements of a great Persian palace partly restored, Persia itself remains almost virgin soil—"an unworked Eldorado."

In the Indus Valley the mysterious civilization of Mohendjodaro cries aloud to be explored. Dating back more

Harp from grave of Queen Shub-ad at Ur
(Courtesy of University Museum, Philadelphia)

than four thousand years, what story has it to tell? What were its connections with the Sumerian civilization with which it was in every way comparable? Certain unusual sealstones found on Sumerian sites have been traced back to Mohendjodaro, where great numbers of them were made. Did both cultures perhaps have a common source?

Only very lately has impenetrable Asia begun to break the silence of its past. Mongolia, Turkestan, Siberia—those are worlds indeed to conquer. An immense wealth of material is to be unearthed there. In Siberia especially where the frost has acted like the bone-dry soil of Egypt and has preserved things just as perfectly. In 1924 and 1925 two hundred tombs were found just south of Lake Baikal. They belonged perhaps to the first century B. C. Though some had been robbed, the trappings of a rich nomad chief—gold plaques, bronze ornaments, wooden carvings, lacquer and embroidered cloth—showed, to everybody's immense surprise, what a high state of civilization nomads can reach.

Africa has much to reveal besides what Egypt has done and will do. Where are the Greek and Carthaginian cities that once flourished on the north coast? And what of the Bantu, that African tribe that built the strange temple of Zimbabwe?

The Far East has scarcely been stirred. What is the story of the Khmer, whose great temple of Angkor, swallowed by the jungle of Cochin-China, was rescued a few years ago? And what of the Polynesians and the riddle of Easter Island?

Last but not least, the New World waits to be conquered once more. In the Maya region alone there is work for a hundred years, and the Maya is by no means the only civilization in the Americas to be rescued and understood. At a hundred different sites archaeologists are at work, and one day—far off as yet—we shall have the whole story. We shall know definitely when man came to the New World and how much he knew when he came. We shall know how he spread over the continents and how he adapted himself to every new condition; where the so-called "maize culture" began, how it spread and how it gave birth to the advanced civilizations of the Americas. And we shall know how, without any influence from the Old World, one of the great races of man rose from savagery to a high degree of civilization.

The second conquest of the earth is a slow, patience-consuming job that has its trials and many disappointments as well as its rich rewards. But the lure of archaeology is very strong. It has the fascination of the detective story, the charm of the jigsaw puzzle. In a thousand out-of-the-way places men and women cheerfully "scorn delights and live laborious days" that they may coax one more secret from the earth. For to them there is no story so absorbing as the Story of Man, no triumph like adding one more page to history.

Some Books to Read

TROY–MYCENAE–CRETE

Baikie, James. *Ancient Crete, the Sea-Kings' Eyrie*. London, 1924.

Baikie, James. *The Sea-Kings of Crete*. London, 1926.

Ludwig, Emil. *Schliemann; the Story of a Gold-Seeker*. Boston, 1931.

Schliemann, Heinrich. *Ilios*. New York, 1881. (This book contains an autobiography.)

EGYPT

Baikie, James. *A Century of Excavation in the Land of the Pharaohs*. New York, 1924.

Carter, Howard. *The Tomb of Tut-ankh-Amen*. London, New York, 1923.

Edwards, Amelia Ann Blandford. *Pharaohs, Fellahs and Explorers*. New York, 1892.

Metropolitan Museum of Art. *The Private Life of the Ancient Egyptians*. New York, 1935.

Petrie, William Matthew Flinders. *Seventy Years in Archaeology*. New York, 1932.

Petrie, William Matthew Flinders. *Ten Years' Digging in Egypt*. London, 1893.

Weigall, Arthur Edward Pearse Brome. *The Glory of the Pharaohs*. London, 1923.

ASSYRIA–BABYLONIA–SUMER

Layard, Austen Henry. *Nineveh and Its Remains*. New York, 1853.

Trotter, Eleanor. *Life in Olden Times in Babylon and Assyria*. London, 1913.

Woolley, Charles Leonard. *The Sumerians*. Oxford, 1929.

Woolley, Charles Leonard. *Ur of the Chaldees, a Record of Seven Years of Excavation*. London, 1929.

MAYA

Gann, Thomas. *Discoveries and Adventures in Central America*. London, 1928.

Gann, Thomas. *Maya Cities, a Record of Exploration and Adventure in Middle America*. London, 1927.

Landa, Diego de. *Yucatan before and after the Conquest, with Other Related Documents*. Translated with notes by William Gates. Baltimore, 1937.

Morris, Ann Axtell. *Digging in Yucatan*. New York, 1931.

Morris, Earl Halstead. *The Temple of the Warriors*. New York, 1931.

Stephens, John Lloyd. *Incidents of Travel in Central America, Chiapas, and Yucatan*. New York, 1841.

Thompson, Edward Herbert. *People of the Serpent*. New York, 1932.

Willard, Theodore Arthur. *The City of the Sacred Well*. New York and London, 1926.

HERE AND THERE IN ARCHAEOLOGY

Baikie, James. *The Glamour of Near East Excavation*. London, 1927.

Magoffin, Ralph Van Deman. *Magic Spades*. New York, 1929.

Masters, David. *The Romance of Excavation*. New York, 1923.

Radin, Paul. *The Story of the American Indian*. New York, 1934.

Woolley, Charles Leonard. *Dead Towns and Living Men*. Oxford, 1920.

Index